Nine Secrets
of Perfect
Horsemanship

Other books by Don Blazer

The Match
Walter Spills The Oats
Natural Western Riding
Make Money With Horses
Healthy Horses Seldom Burp
Training The Western Show Horse
Horses Don't Care About Women's Lib

Nine Secrets of Perfect Horsemanship

Don Blazer

First Edition
Second printing

Editor, Meribah Small
Cover art by Janie White

www.donblazer.com
Success Is Easy, Scottsdale, Arizona

Published by **Success Is Easy**
13610 N. Scottsdale Road
Suite 10-406.
Scottsdale, AZ 85331
www.donblazer.com

First published as a Success Is Easy paperback 1998
Second printing 2001

Library of Congress Catalog Card number 97-91294

ISBN 0-9660127-1-2

Printed in the United States of America

Taylor Ashleigh Hanson
follow your heart

Table of Contents

Introduction
Nine secrets revealed   9

Chapter one
The promise is within   11

Chapter two
The heart answers   31

Chapter three
Three guides: slow, low, no   49

Chapter four
Giving is a perfect act   65

Chapter five
Choose to know the truth   81

Chapter six
Everything is exactly right   99

Chapter seven
You control your future   117

Chapter eight
Surrender to uncertainty   135

Chapter nine
Require nothing. Give everything   151

Introduction
Nine secrets revealed

The secrets of perfect horsemanship are not new; in fact they are ancient wisdom, known, if not always expressed, by the world's true horsemen.

Knowing the secrets focuses the mind on the connections between horse and rider and brings their energies into harmony.

When the secrets are revealed to the superior horseman, he opens his mind and uses the secrets.

Lesser horsemen close their minds, and ignore or laugh at the secrets. They are afraid to take responsibility for their actions.

When gimmicks or tricks are offered as a shortcut to horsemanship, lesser horsemen are quick to embrace them. The promise of fast cures or equipment miracles are dismissed with good humor by superior horsemen.

When information is offered to improve horsemanship, its value can only be validated in practice. So it is with the secrets. They must be studied, accepted and applied. Then their truth can be known.

Then perfection in horsemanship is attained.

Each has a dream. The creative potential to make it
come true lies within. Accept your power.

Chapter one
The promise is within

I promise you the understanding and the experience of perfection, championships if they are your goal, the pure joy of the partnership between horse and rider, and successes which at this moment you think are unattainable dreams. Your dreams will be your reality tomorrow.

I promise you horses which respond to the lightest cue, that jump, race, rein or event at world class levels. I promise you horses ready, willing and able to be your complete and equal partner.

I promise you the nine secrets of perfect horsemanship and the six elements of horse training, which when used in synergy can solve any training or riding problem.

To enjoy my promise, you must promise me your dedication.

Cathy was 14-years-old when she said, "I want to ride at the World."

She was referring to the American Quarter

Chapter one

Horse Association World Championships. To ride at the World Championships, you must be invited. And to be invited, you must earn qualifying points by competing and winning or placing at recognized Quarter Horse shows around the country.

There is a youth division in Quarter Horse competition, and there is a Youth World Championship event, but these didn't interest her at the time. She wanted to take on the best horses and the nation's top trainers at the World.

And of course she did.

Two years later, she competed at the World, even though by establishment standards she never should have been there.

She was just a kid, riding a nondescript, ranch-bred brown gelding, whose breeding certainly wasn't fashionable. But she was there, taking on the best, and reaching her own perfection. Her dream, as she had envisioned it, was now her reality.

Was it a big deal that she accomplished so much?

No!

She only did what hundreds of others in her circumstances have done before and since. She simply applied, without ever being aware she was doing so, one of the secrets of perfect horsemanship.

She had the intention of riding at the World Championships. When she decided to compete, and when she envisioned the competition in her mind, leaving only the certainty that she would, she foreordained the event when she took her first action toward achieving her goal.

It had to happen. And of course it did.

Our every thought, idea, dream can become our reality if we take the actions to make them so.

Cathy's thought, idea and dream was to compete at the world championships. And that is what she did--compete.

At the time, she did not have as a goal the winning of a world championship, or even being placed in the top ten. Had she had those higher ambitions, she would have had to apply many of the other secrets, and in doing so, would have traveled a very different path with maybe a very different horse. It might have taken her longer, and she surely would have experienced many different events along the way. But no matter how it may have come about, the achievement of even those goals would have been as inevitable. Whatever is expressed in thought is possible.

What you can conceive, you can achieve.

The thought, idea or dream is always at first expressed as a completed picture. You desire a final result. You name it and visualize it.

To convert the thought, idea or dream into reality requires you to take an action. It is when you take the first action toward the reality of your dream that your conception begins to divide into individual steps, singular goals, and the next action. It is the individual steps, the actions taken, the goals attained and unattained which are the lessons propelling you to your assured destiny.

You have the ability to reach any goal you choose. The ability is within you; it is a part of you.

Chapter one

It has been given; it cannot be taken away.

This ability, this creative potential within all of us, is an infinite intelligence--the source, God, the force, nature, the Tao, the unknown and unnamed. It does not matter what you call it, or if you call it nothing.

It is there; it is a part of you, just as you are a part of it.

If this is starting to sound like a religious sermon, it is not. This has nothing to do with religion. There are no rituals to be performed in order to be part of this power. You join nothing. Nothing is required of you. The power is a gift given at the moment of your creation. You were, before your present life form, as you are now, creative potential.

Throughout the history of mankind, it has been known there is this power--this infinite intelligence which transcends our understanding and comprehension. Ancient man called the power by many names, made it many gods, worshipped it in many ways and sought to gain its grace. As man came to know more about his world and universe, thought divided into science and religion. Science was atheistic because it was capable of arriving at explanations for complex and abstract ideas and events. Science was positive that based on previously correct conclusions, eventually it would be able to explain all. Religious men, on the other hand, believed in a God, the power behind all things, and leaped the unexplainable by faith.

All things change, and today's science now

acknowledges the unexplainable without denying the existence of an energy beyond understanding.

Infinite intelligence (that force beyond understanding) rules every galaxy, the universes, every atom, every sub-atom, every cell within our being and the life force which is our horse.

Nothing is by chance, nothing is random; everything has a purpose and a function, a direction and a goal.

Science can prove that we and everything we believe to exist are just a few simple elements. We, and all the animals and insects and plants and mountains and rivers of the earth, are just different combinations of those same elements. Science has proven and we understand that everything is nothing more than thousands, millions, billions, trillions of molecules vibrating at various speeds. Our billions of vibrating molecules create our forms, which are not solid, and which are not the true "us." The true "you" is the creative potential, the spirit, which is contained within your form. The true you is the creative potential which allows you to think, to have ideas, to dream.

That true you is a life force, and it is the same life force which is the truth of your horse.

Your DNA (deoxyribonucleic acid), is the program created by your life force, and the DNA of your horse is the program of its life force. Those of science who categorize all things within the universe will say there are observable differences between the DNA of you and your horse, and therefore you are not the same. And while it is true the programs create forms which are different, when taken to the essence--the life force--there is no difference. Life is life. The infinite intelligence which is life creates different programs resulting in different forms. Still, the life force in all things remains the same. You are one with all things in the universe; you are one with your horse. There can be no separation.

It is because there can be no true separation from anything within our universe--no separation from our horses--that we can experience a partnership of perfection.

For millenniums our forefathers have recognized our sameness with all things. They called the horse and all animals our brothers and sisters.

Ancients spoke with nature by being silent and listening to the sunrise. They understood there is a connection between all things. There has always been the wisdom that each of us, that each thing, is an equal and integral part of all that is. Nothing is greater; nothing is less.

Because of this connection, there have been horsemen throughout time, who were capable of using their creative potential at will to transcend form and recognize their oneness with the horse. The stories of such horsemen have been told for nearly four thousand years.

I know today there are many more such horsemen, and I know you too can experience such a transformation.

You have the creative potential, and it is unlimited.

You can create any reality you choose. You

can, by the choice of your own free will, direct your potential to take over your life and transform any thought, idea or dream into your existence. Nothing is unachievable. Everything is possible.

Knowing, and then allowing your potential to take control, is not a matter of thinking positively. Positive thinking and visualization (psycho cybernetics) are limited in scope and success. They are simply thoughts defined. The true power, your creative potential, is the infinite intelligence which makes it possible to have thoughts, ideas, dreams.

Positive thinking will bring results. Psycho cybernetics (mind-visualization) is a step toward using your potential. But such thinking is a mental exercise, and thereby limited to "thinking." Thinking always calls for judgments--things are good or bad, correct or incorrect, positive or negative, right or wrong.

Creative potential does not make judgments.

Man's mind is limited to differentiating, evaluating and/or naming things. Therefore, the mind always constricts, restrains and limits.

Creative potential is beyond the mind. It is beyond thinking. Creative potential is the power of non-thinking; it is the power of absolute knowing. And it is this knowing which makes the future a reality in this moment.

Creative potential is inexhaustible and free.

Creative potential is in your heart rather than your mind, and you must accept it in order to free it.

To reassure yourself your creative potential exists, to know and see it in your heart, reflect on

17

experiences you have had with horses. Undoubtedly there have been times when you have known exactly what to do with a horse at exactly the correct moment just because it simply felt right. Logic, the use of the mind, was not involved. The feeling was beyond the mind. It was a knowing.

There have been occasions when you knew a horse would shy from something even before it happened. Your thought came intuitively. There have also been times when you have been so close to a horse, so in tune with a horse, that you could trust him to do exactly as you wanted at the moment. You did not go through the process of thinking logically what could have, should have or would have been if......

It was not a mental exercise.

Such understanding was your creative potential endowing you with correct action without thought--your potential making you and the horse one.

You knew.

The knowing was in your heart, not your mind.

You do not have to see it, touch it, taste it, smell it or hear it to know it exists.

I have explained that any thought, any idea, any dream can become your reality, so you must choose carefully how you direct your creative potential. Your intentions and desires, even if not well-planned, will manifest themselves. If you focus on the things which you perceive as wrong, those are the events which become your reality over and over again.

You are exactly where you are, based on the actions you have taken to fulfill your intentions and desires.

As you proceed toward the realization of your dreams and ideas, events will occur which do not at first seem relevant. Be assured, even the events which your mind labels as "wrong" are the events you have created, and they have purpose.

The exact meaning or importance of each happening on the way to conclusion may not be easy to understand, but there is a lesson. Search for and concentrate on the lesson, not on the path, for the road you travel, no matter its twists and turns, leads to the destiny you have expressed.

Clearly define your desires and give conscious thought to your intentions, so your creative potential can more directly bring about what you truly want. If you let sloppy thoughts direct your potential, you will experience events you had no idea you requested. This can lead to confusion, frustration and doubt. It has happened to all of us, and it slows our journey.

At a relatively early age I believed "As ye think, so shall ye be." The problem was, I didn't always give conscious consideration to my thought. (Too frequently, I still don't). And so I needed a little demonstration (a lesson) to jolt me into the recognition of my creative potential at work.

The first time I actually reviewed and retraced, step by step, my potential at work was a short time after my introduction to a four-year-old stallion.

19

Chapter one

I had been told the horse was a rogue, but at the time I was young and quite confident I could ride anything with a mane and a tail. My confidence, however, began evaporating a moment or two after the horse arrived at my ranch.

I was helping the horse back out of the trailer by first putting my hand on his hip, then along his side as he moved backward. The instant his front feet were out of the trailer, he turned toward me and struck with his right front foot. As it crashed to the ground, his unshod hoof scraped my forehead, then my nose. The sunglasses I had been wearing were crumpled in the dirt under his hoof, my nose and forehead now bloodied.

In that instant I knew I would have trouble with this horse. (Amazing insight!) It was the knowing which was to be my pain. Knowing brings the future into the present moment.

I directed my creative potential toward perceived trouble. Rather than seeking the lesson from the experience by giving thought to what had happened and why it had occurred, I chose to leap to the negative and allow my creative potential to guarantee the future would be stormy.

The future arrived the next morning when I went out to ride the horse. (He was, I had been told, broke to ride.) As I stood and looked at this strong, chunky Appaloosa, I knew in my heart he would buck me off. I was not aware of thinking that he would buck me off, but I knew just the same it would happen.

Since I was unaware of my ability to direct my

creative potential, I never gave a thought to the idea I could make choices and thereby changes in what I then considered unavoidable. I had no idea I could make an immediate difference in the eventual outcome. I accepted my first vision of the future, and thereby allowed my creative potential to bring it to reality. I sealed my fate.

I saddled up.

The horse didn't buck me off once. He bucked me off three or four times that day and a couple of more times the next day.

Being on the ground more than I was on the horse, and not being so anxious for the next body bruising, I passed most of those two days in quiet contemplation. I wanted a way out of this battle.

Finally the thought struck me that I had anticipated trouble, so trouble was what I got.

I concluded I had been focused on having trouble with the horse rather than on reschooling the horse. I was beginning to understand.

My body was sore, so it was not to hard to convince myself I needed a new approach.

I decided if I chose not to have further trouble with the horse, I could eliminate trouble. I would avoid trouble no matter how it presented itself. I focused only on each step of reschooling.

I began a completely new relationship with the horse.

I started at the very beginning, proceeding as if the horse had never been touched. My purpose now was not just to ride the horse and reschool him, but to ride and reschool him without problems. My creative potential now had new, better defined direction.

Progress was swift.

Remember, creative potential is infinite and inexhaustible, and brings about every scene, every minor and major event, every moment within our lives.

Being consciously aware of my intention, I gave definitive direction to my creative potential. It was a done deal. I would ride the horse--without force, without a fight--by being one with him. Whatever was going to be, I would accept without resistance.

At the moment, he was not ready to be ridden, so I spent several days working with him on the ground, driving, longeing, grooming, working at leading, standing and loading in a trailer.

In a couple of days I knew in my heart he was willing to be ridden. There was nothing special about the moment. I just knew.

So I rode the horse because I knew I could ride him, and because I was ready to ride him and because he was ready to be ridden.

It was a wonderful experience.

But it also became a problem!

My ego inflated.

Even though I had been given a small introductory view of my creative potential, I was without complete understanding. I was then, as we all are most often, directed by my ego. It was more natural and more comfortable to simply believe my mind and body could control all circumstances. It was easy to listen to my ego which always concerns itself with your form, which is your body, your physical self.

My ego began telling me how great I was now that my body had ridden the horse. I was, at the time, willing to accept the idea my body, rather than my creative potential, controlled the horse. I foolishly listened to my ego. And because I listened, I didn't recognize my creative potential again for months.

The physical self, which is the obsession of the ego, is not the real you, but is the self which is put on display in front of the judges of a western pleasure class, a dressage test or a hunt seat competition. This is the self you believe others see. This is the image your parents, peers and 10 million advertisements try to direct you to be--the self your ego wants you to be.

The ego, which is very shallow, believes that it is extremely important no one ever sees your form in a compromising or foolish position, whatever it may be. The ego makes you depressed, nervous, angry or defensive if it believes for a second you are being perceived as anything less than wonderful. The ego doesn't recognize the fact that most people don't notice you at all.

If your ego is in control, you become frustrated and angry and behave ridiculously when your horse's actions are not the ones you wanted, expected or planned.

But your ego is not the true you. It is just a collection of all the negative ideas we have about ourselves, and about everyone else.

The great philosophers and religious leaders have for centuries lectured, "know thy self."

The real you, as you are learning, is beyond your form and beyond your mind. The real you is your creative potential--your ability to do anything. The real you is eternal spirit, infinite intelligence and energy, which can neither be created nor destroyed.

To better understand examples of the difference between the mind and potential, reflect on scenes you have witnessed or perhaps been a part of.

How many times have you watched competitors get ready to enter a class, and as they prepared their horse and themselves, you heard in conversation and saw in actions the ego dominate? If the ego was in control, directing the person's actions, you heard the rider criticize the horse, or the judges or the grounds. If the ego was in control, the rider may have expressed nervousness, temper, anger, bewilderment, or may openly have predicted his impending poor showing.

However, if the creative potential was being allowed to flow unimpeded, the rider was sure to be quiet, exuding confidence in both himself and the horse. Such positive behavior was expressed since there was no need for nervousness or worry because creative potential predetermined the performance was to be everything the horse and rider were prepared to give.

And the rider was willing to accept the result, knowing the result could only be what it should be at that particular time and place.

Remember, creative potential is beyond the mind--it is infinite intelligence. Creative potential is not comprehensible to the mind because the mind is limited. Creative potential is unlimited and always correct. Creative potential is in your heart and the heart has no fear.

The mind gives rise to your ego. Your ego always seeks two things: the approval of others and control of others. The ego is based in fear. The ego remains with the mind and avoids the heart.

Gloria, a friend, a psychologist and a relatively new horseowner, told me that in her first contact with horses she sensed there was a spiritual aspect to the relationship. She described it as an energy which "is completely evident and real."

She added that her work in psychology shows her nearly everyone is able to be in touch with or aware of that other dimension of life. Of course, she is referring to the unseen creative potential which dwells in your heart.

"I am so honored to have horses in my life," Gloria continued, "and to be able to grow and become aware of my true relationship to nature, and to see that we--man and animals--are each and all just simply energies in the field."

Gloria suggests one of the easiest ways to recognize whether ego or creative potential is directing you is to review or be aware of your behavior.

"If you are angry, defensive, critical or are trying to control others," she explained, "ego is in control. "On the other hand, if you accept the moment, are kind, gentle, forgiving and trusting, your heart is in control."

Ego seeks domination and control. Horse training too often is under the direction of ego, which gives rise to the idea the horse must be under control in any situation. The truth is just the opposite. The heart is stronger than the ego, and when the horse is given freedom, asked instead of controlled, perfection results.

Remember, softness always defeats hardness, bending always withstands, while stiffness cracks. Throughout history, violence has always been overcome by the redirection of violence. The horse responds to firmness as a form of love, but always recoils from pain--never giving, only submitting.

Let me caution you that even when you become aware of your creative potential, it is difficult to remain in focus because your mind keeps vying for your attention with thoughts and ideas and worries and concerns. And all of those thoughts and ideas and worries have to do with your form--your body--and what people will think of it, and how it looks on a horse. Worse, when you are training a horse, and your ego is leading the way, you are always seeking control over the horse rather than oneness with his spirit.

Regrettably, all this confusion going on in your head effectively keeps you from reaching your true self.

It is hard to get past thinking and simply accept our own creative potential because our minds are constantly being bombarded with messages telling you to think a certain way, to act a certain way, to be forever on the go, striving, reaching for goals. But most of the goals being pushed into your consciousness are worthless.

What material things are really of true worth? None can last. Once held, they lose value. Yet the striving goes on. Still, no matter how much a person acquires, he can never get enough of what he doesn't need.

No commerce, no society, no government can enhance your natural ability, can give greater quality to life, can provide self worth, can allow you to be one with the universe. Only you can find your true self and live in the potential, your creative potential--the infinite intelligence of all things.

To find your creative potential, stop all noise.

To find your creative potential, seek a quiet place and be quiet. Stop talking and begin listening, listening for the sounds of silence.

You do not have to be entertained. Instead of being entertained, do nothing, but concentrate on your desires and intentions.

You do not have to be hard at work. Your potential works without action by you.

You can await the results quietly.

Silence seemed to be the single secret Doug used to train all his winners. A tall, lanky, slow-moving fellow from Ohio, Doug has trained many champions. He would ride a horse for a few minutes, asking for a single response. If the horse made an attempt to respond correctly, he would stop the horse and sit quietly. When he thought the horse had had plenty of time to absorb the lesson, he would start riding again. He would ride for a few more minutes, then stop, and remain quiet.

When I asked him about his technique, he replied, "I just let the silence and stillness do the work for me."

In the silence you can decide what it is you want--how much of the promise you are willing to accept, and how much you are willing to dedicate. You may only want a responsive horse, or you may wish simply to compete on the local level. Maybe you will seek a world championship, or a place as a member of an Olympic team, or strive to be an instructor or the trainer of the horse considered the greatest of all time in his field.

The choices are yours.

When you do accept your creative potential and discover your ability to use it at will, do not be pleased with yourself, thinking you are special, or better or smarter than anyone else.

You are not!

Everyone has creative potential. Everyone is the creation of infinite intelligence.

You are special in the same way everyone is special.

You simply know of your potential and are exactly where you should be in this universe. You are no more and no less than anyone else.

Because you are where you are now, you know the FIRST SECRET of training and reaching perfect horsemanship: YOUR CREATIVE POTENTIAL

EXISTS. ACCEPT IT.

By accepting your creative potential, you also accept responsibility for yourself. How you react to what happens to you is by your choice. You make the decisions; you take the actions to create your reality.

You achieve all that you conceive.

Do not be afraid to dream. Dare to be great.

You are alone and responsible for yourself, and at the same time, never alone, but one with all that exists.

You are creative potential. You are the promise.

Your heart always speaks true. Follow the truth. No
matter the distance, stay the course.

Chapter two
The heart answers

I promised you the secrets of perfect horsemanship, and in return, I've asked for your promise of dedication.

I told you the first secret--your creative potential exists, accept it and accept responsibility for yourself.

Now it is time for you to take four actions.

1. Decide what and who you are.

2. Decide what you want to achieve.

3. Evaluate your horse's physical and mental abilities.

4. Determine the extent of your dedication.

You know you have the power and intelligence within you to achieve whatever you can conceive. You can choose to take on any activity, any competition. But do you have the form--the physical qualities necessary to facilitate the performance? Will your physical traits make it easier or more difficult to succeed?

No one has perfect physical qualities for all

types of riding and training. What is advantageous for one discipline is often less suitable for another. But no matter what your physical form, there is some equine activity for you.

We all need to condition and maintain our bodies to perform at maximum potential. If you have physical limitations, take action to minimize them, but recognize and accept them. Now focus on the riding or training styles for which your physical form is most suited.

In general, a slender figure of medium build is desirable for a rider or trainer. The anatomy of a distance runner or dancer is also best for a show rider. A trainer is blessed if he or she has a similar build. However, being a little heavier won't hurt.

The long-legged rider/trainer has a physical advantage since most control cues are given by leg aids and body-weight shifts. The long-legged rider can more easily get his or her legs on the horse, thus maintaining a deeper seat and better balance.

The rider's essential base of support consists of the thighs and pelvis, which are connected at the hip joint. If the pelvis is low and narrow, the center of gravity is low and more stable, no matter the height of the upper body. Long legs tend to stabilize the rider, reducing unwanted upper body movement. Long legs also make it easier for the rider to squeeze the horse forward.

The rider should sit down on a horse as if being lowered straight down from a crane, thus making the major points of contact the seat and inner surface of the thighs. A natural flat thigh is perfect. Riders with heavy thighs will have difficulty maintaining a deep seat, driving a horse forward, keeping the knees close to the horse and keeping the heels down with the foot parallel to the horse's side. Exercises to flatten the thighs may be one of the desired body improvements.

Straight legs, neither knock-kneed nor bowlegged, are also a great asset for the performance horse rider. In any performance event, especially those involving speed, the knees must be kept solid against the horse. When turning the toe out and the heel in for placement of a precise cue, the knee should be relaxed and may come away from the horse for the length of time it takes to complete the communication. The proper knee position is the result of sitting straight down on the horse (straddling), rather than sitting with knees forward as if on a couch.

A large or heavy upper body is not helpful, nor are high shoulders, since they raise the center of gravity, making it more difficult to maintain balance. Riders with heavy upper bodies also tend to throw their horses out of balance with rapid and often unwanted weight shifts.

A good straight spine (a spine approaching a flat shape) can better assume and maintain an upright posture.

If you are a small person, with short legs and a muscular upper body, reining horses may not be for you. But there is no reason you can't carefully and thoughtfully position a western trail horse to clear all obstacles.

If you are slight and lack strength, you may not want to compete in three-day events or in open jumping. But there is no reason you can't master an English, western pleasure or dressage test.

You may not have the perfect body for one specific activity, but there are other activities for which you are very well suited.

When choosing a style of riding or training, certainly your physical form should be considered. Physical limitations can be overcome, but at what cost? Are you willing to pay?

Consider what you are (form) to determine what physical activities will be easiest and most comfortable for you.

Then consider who you are. This involves a truthful look at your personality and character traits. What kind of activities stress you? Do you thrive on competition, or do you prefer quiet solitude? In considering these things, recognize that you can change much of who you are by changing the way you think. But change is not always easy, so you must factor in the amount of dedication required to become who and what you want to be.

Both what you are (physical form) and who you are (mental makeup) affect what you can and can't easily do as an equestrian.

Regardless of the obstacles, in the final analysis, your choice of a riding or training style must be your heart's desire.

If your heart chooses, then it will be a choice of passion. And any effort directed by your creative potential and driven by passion will overcome any limitation.

Simply knowing you cannot fail does not mean you should deliberately choose what appears physically impossible. That is not the way to test your creative potential. That would be an ego choice, not a choice of the heart.

In trying to learn your heart's desire, there will be hundreds of opinions, suggestions and pressures--some saying you can't and some saying you should or must. Evaluate, consider, but listen only to your heart. Your heart will not be swayed. Your heart knows what is right for you.

Do not listen to your ego. You cannot choose for the approval you will receive, and you must not choose expecting money or benefits in return. The expectation of what you will get for your effort is not your heart's way.

Your heart's desire is love, and if you do something because you listened to your heart, you will do it without the need for praise or financial reward. That which is done for love has its reward in the doing, and all other needs will be provided.

If you don't truly love doing something, don't choose to do it. Even when you love what you are doing, there will be frustrations, trials, setbacks, and pain. Many tasks in themselves will not be enjoyable, but you will do them because they are a part of the whole--the thing you love.

External pressures and the expressed opinions of others may cause you to think you should do a particular thing with horses, but only when your heart says, "yes" will the choice be correct. If your heart does not agree with your mind, you must go with your heart and say "no" to your ego-driven mind which is seeking peer approval or control.

Remember, physical talent is not the guiding force. Physical talent is helpful, but not necessarily required. It is not even necessary that you take a major physical role in the event you choose.

Your heart may insist you would really love to instruct or coach another to a jumping championship. Maybe you will be driven by a passion to condition race horses. I've known several race horse trainers confined to wheelchairs, and still they have been very successful at their chosen work.

When you choose your heart's desire, happiness and fulfillment confirm your corrrect choice.

Don't worry about the specifics of how you will accomplish the job. If the desire comes from the heart, your creative potential will take control and what is necessary for accomplishment will be provided. New tools and new systems will be designed and invented to help you. Miracles will happen.

No matter what event or competition you decide upon, and no matter what role you intend to play, there are some helpful hints which can smooth the way.

Join an association or club which sanctions, or is actively involved with the competition or work you seek. The association will have copies of the rules governing the events which interest you, and descriptions of the horsemanship levels expected. The association generally will keep you updated on the latest activities by newsletter or magazine.

By selecting certain areas of horsemanship, you become involved, and in so doing, your interest will propel you to gain knowledge. It's fun, it's easy, it's the way it should be. If you have chosen well, it will never be a chore, be boring, or depressing work.

If you are not already participating as a competitor, attend competitions as a spectator, an observer, a seeker of perfection, thirsting for a complete understanding of what it takes to reach the goals you have selected.

Don't be afraid to ask questions.

Horsemen love to talk about their horses and tell stories about their successes. Listen carefully and learn. This is not the time to expound your theories, but it is the time to grasp the nuances between experiencing perfection, winning, and just competing. Listen and give a hearty thanks to those who are helping you to reach perfect horsemanship, for they, too, are practicing a secret.

As you become more and more knowledgeable about your chosen activity, you will also be learning a great deal about the type of horse it takes to carry you to your goal. Every competition is unique, yet similar to every other competition. Each horse is unique, yet similar. It is the differences between horses, competition to competition, winners to losers, which you must recognize.

Whatever the activity you've selected, it is the

37

horse which must perform to perfection if you are to reach the goal and victory. You can make mistakes; most of them won't be seen. But the horse is always in the spotlight, and the mistakes of the horse are what every judge, every competitor and every spectator is waiting to catch.

Avoid mistakes by always making it as easy as possible for the horse to perform the task asked. Keep in mind that selecting proper conformation for a particular event makes it easier for the horse to reach perfection or give a winning performance.

Every event favors a particular type of horse, and while any horse can probably do the event, certain horses are best suited to winning specific competition. Certain breeds of horses are especially adapted to winning at particular sports--the Thoroughbred for flat racing and steeple chasing, the Quarter Horse for cutting and as a working cow horse, the Arabian for long distance competition such as "ride and tie."

Styles and fads make certain breeds of horses popular for certain events. In selecting a breed of horse, you want to be sure it will be in vogue during your competitive years. Knowledge you have gained through involvement with an association and by attending competitions as an observer or competitor will give you an edge in selecting your horse.

A good-looking horse will always have a slight advantage in any competition. A well-conformed horse will have fewer soundness problems and more useful years.

If the horse has a finely-chiselled, lean head

he'll make a great first impression. Leanness is evidence of mobility and nerve, while wide nostrils and a wide jaw at the throatlatch are necessary to give the horse great energy and breathing power.

A large, soft eye is one of the principal attributes of a good head. The calm, fully-colored eye reflects the horse's good disposition and should give you confidence. Ears set close to the top of the head and forward, are a sign of good breeding, evidence of sensitivity and an ability to learn.

Not all breeds of horses have picture perfect heads, but all good performance horses have the essentials. Avoid horses with wild eyes, long floppy ears, or restricted air passages.

The horse's neck should be long and free, wide in the gullet and thin and refined at the throatlatch. You want the crest to be slightly curved upward, and the bottom line to be straight. Short, heavy necks set low on the shoulders do not aid equilibrium, making fast performance work difficult for the horse.

The preferred set of the neck will be determined by the event you have chosen. Fads and fashion will dictate certain conformations to be more advantageous at certain times. Training can often help the neck carriage, but it can't offset a fad.

Low, short withers do not provide a good base for any saddle. Mutton-withered horses should be passed.

A long, forward sloping shoulder is usually desirable. It helps give the horse fluidity in motion. On the other hand, if an event calls for a "shuffle" at certain gaits, then a short, upright shoulder is needed.

The length of the horse's arm must be suitable for the job to be done. If a long-striding step is wanted, then the arm should connect to the shoulder at right angles. If elevated, halting strides are desirable, the arm should attach at an angle greater than 90 degrees.

If a horse is expected to do a lot of fast work, or a lot of rapid turns and rollbacks, then the elbow joint should be separated from the side of the chest by at least a finger's width.

The forearm should be long, compared to the cannon, and both should have plenty of bone. The tendons along the cannon bone should be strong and extremely well-defined.

The knee should be low, flat and of good size. There should be no puffiness around the knee, nor around the clean, lean fetlock joint.

The desired length and angle of the pastern is almost always determined by the needed action of a horse for the competition he is to perform. Too long and sloping a pastern lengthens stride but often results in soundness problems. A steep pastern shortens length of stride, but also frequently results in unsoundness. A moderate, strong, elastic pastern is probably the best all-around choice.

The hoof will be a problem area for the life of the horse. Few horsemen care for the hoof of the young horse properly, and almost none care correctly for the shod hoof of the performance horse.

Do not leave the care of your horse's feet to

your farrier. If you seek perfect horsemanship, you are responsible.

The hoof should be of moderate size in relation to the size of the horse. Avoid horses with extra large, flat, narrow, boxy, clubbed feet or contracted heels. Any of these conditions are extremely difficult to keep healthy during a heavy performance campaign.

Once the horse is shod, the health of the hoof is apt to deteriorate. The best which can be hoped for is a good maintenance program and a cooperative farrier.

The toe should be kept short, the heels wide and open, the frog well-trimmed and barely touching the ground. The soles should be slightly concave.

The length of the horse's back should be moderate. Short-coupled horses, while satisfactory for some events, are generally too stiff and rigid. The length of the back is the combined result of the withers, the backbone and a strong loin. Avoid sway backed or hog backed horses.

A "square" horse--one in which the distance from the shoulder to the pelvis is not greater than the height at the withers--will always have difficulty with balance due to the shortness of the area of support.

Narrow-chested horses lack stamina, since they don't have enough room for the heart and lungs to function efficiently during strenuous work.

The hindquarters are extremely important to any performance horse, since all action initiates in the hindquarters. You want a performance horse to be long between the hip and buttocks and between the hip joint and the stifle joint. The stifle joint should be well forward. There should also be plenty of length between the stifle joint and the hock. A low hock is a good sign of power and speed, and provides for a short hind cannon bone. The hock should be large and strong, with well-defined bones and ligaments which blend well into the cannon.

Sickle, or cow-hocked horses do not have as much thrust power as a horse with a straight hind leg. However, such horses are often very useful in minimum stress events.

If a horse has good hindquarters, he will easily over stride his front foot print with his hind foot when he is at a natural free walk.

The color of a horse is of little importance when it comes to performance, but perhaps it can give you an edge when it comes to winning.

Statistically, the gray horse will win much more often when his performance is equal or just slightly below that of the best performer. In classes where the horse is given credit for smoothness, grace and overall appearance, the gray will have a 17 percent better chance of winning.

Now who bothers to figure out such unimportant matters? Those who know who they are and what they want and have dedicated themselves to that goal. Study the color of champions of the event you have chosen so you'll know when you want a bay horse without socks or one with a large blaze.

The size of a horse is not very important when

it comes to performance ability, but of great importance when it comes to following current fads. The big horse fad comes and goes about every 50 to 100 years. Study the history of horses and you will note the big horse has the popular vote until the little horse out-performs him. Then the smaller horse reigns for a short period of time until larger men and women begin another trend for larger horses.

Suffice to say, it is difficult to be under-mounted and easy to be over-mounted. If you need a mounting block, you're over-mounted, have chosen the wrong horse or are in the wrong event. Smaller horses perform well at virtually any event and they win more than their fair share. I can agree from experience that a good big horse is better than a good small horse, but I also know from experience there are many more good small horses than there are good big horses.

Jumping is one of those events where the demand for a big horse is a fad to be recognized, but not a necessity. When a horse passes 16 hands in height, his mass grows at a more rapid rate than his muscle strength. As he gets bigger, his size actually makes him weaker. Evaluate a horse's ability to perform the tasks you have selected first, then seek to meet the fad of the day.

Choose a horse because you know he is conformationally correct for the event, not because your ego fears someone's disapproval.

Conformation assets and liabilities will have different degrees of importance based on the event in which your horse will appear. Never fear, even horses with less than perfect conformation will find a place and purpose.

When you know your goal, when it has been defined and refined by specifics, you will be able to describe the horse you want. And since you can now define him in specific terms, you will find him. When you have dedicated yourself to the knowing, there will be no need for supportive opinions by other horsemen, or the pre-purchase approval of a veterinarian. A soundness examination by a veterinarian should tell you what exists and what health or soundness problems need to be addressed. The decision to buy or not is yours, not a veterinarian's. The health and soundness of your horse is your responsibility; assistance and information, not decisions, are to be provided by veterinarians and farriers.

When you've taken a long, hard look at your body's shape and have accepted it, when you are comfortable with who you are, when you have let your heart choose its desire, and when you have learned the assets and liabilities of your horse's physical form, you are ready to assess your dedication.

What have you done to bring yourself to this point?

Your past dedication to projects is a way of evaluating just how prepared you are for this moment. Have you stayed your course, no matter the difficulties, or have you easily been discouraged by problems and troubles? Do you face obstacles and find solutions, or do you quit and take up other interests?

How strong a dedication to winning, to reaching perfection in horsemanship, does your past reveal?

You cannot change your past, but you can accept this moment and challenge yourself to create the future you want.

If your goal is to win some class at some show someday, or to be a little better rider or trainer than you are now, you will get a first place ribbon eventually, and you will improve a bit. When and where you get the ribbon will be "somewhere and sometime". You will have succeeded. You will have reached your goal. You cannot deny you got exactly what you had decided to achieve.

To fulfill a fuzzy, general idea takes little dedication.

A goal of pure clarity......great dedication.

Your dedication determines how much time and effort you must expend.

If you have thoughts about devoting less than 100 percent of yourself, don't choose to be a champion. Don't expect to reach perfection in horsemanship. Great horsemanship--riding and training--requires a love no less than that of a poet. Being the best and one with any endeavor requires total giving. I am not suggesting you can't have a full life and good relationships as well. You can, but expect some difficult personal moments.

Dedication can also be defined as sacrifice.

Your friends will praise the thought and labor

45

you put into reaching your goal. Yet the same effort will be derided by those you surpass.

Your qualities of honesty, loyalty and persistence, will suddenly become stupidity and stubbornness to critics you have just defeated in competition, or to those who believe you have failed them by not providing them as much time and attention as they expected. Of course, it is their ego which directs their opinions.

If you are willing to make sacrifices, then you are willing to accept the glory of achievement.

To gain, you must give away.

By giving away, you will receive.

And you must treat both giving and receiving with the same calm, quiet acceptance.

You will be told how lucky you are to be able to do exactly as you want all the time while being blessed by so much good fortune.

You know the truth.

You have been blessed with no more than anyone else.

Everyone has the same power as you. Everyone can use the power. You are not smarter, braver, or luckier than anyone else. It is simply that you have dedicated yourself to an idea, allowing your power to take you to your chosen place.

How much you want is up to you. Let your heart's desire be your future.

Just a good, pleasant experience with a horse is very often enough. Many are completely satisfied with competing at small shows, just getting along with their horse, winning a ribbon, being considered a good enough rider.

Your heart can tell you when enough is enough.

If in your heart there is room for more than what you have now, great!

You can have it all!

Now is the time to start. Now is the time to do it.

You cannot succeed by thinking positively about the event you have selected.

You must do something about it. Take action.

You cannot succeed by reading, or talking or surrounding yourself with posters of your heroes.

You must get out and get into it. Take action.

You cannot succeed by pretending to be something you are not.

You must be what you want.

Live this moment knowing you are everything you want to be. Living your future starts with a single action, which leads to another action, which leads to several new actions, which move you a tiny bit closer to your goal.

At the time, you may never understand what each action has to do with the final achievement, but each action is a necessary requirement.

Nothing is random, nothing is by chance. You are at this position in life for a reason.

You choose and you send your spirit on a mission.

And while on that mission, throughout your future, use the SECOND SECRET to perfection in horsemanship--LET YOUR HEART DECIDE.

Before the big fences, horse and rider begin low.
Slow in approach, rapid results, no criticism.

Chapter three
Three guides: slow, low, no

You know you have infinite creative potential. Therefore, all your dreams are possible.

You know if you follow your heart, you will always make the correct choice.

Secrets to perfection--miracles in life.

Before another secret, a rule and three guidelines to the training of horses.

This book is about finding perfection in horsemanship. Perfection is doing the very best you possibly can at a specific moment, and knowing you have done your very best.

This book is not about the specifics of training methods or styles or disciplines that pertain to particular equestrian events.

What you want to do, and how you want to do it are up to you. Styles or disciplines are personal choices. None is more or less correct than any other. All are simply choices.

Chapter three

How you participate is also just a personal choice. Perfection is wherever you find it. You may want to be a trainer, or you may wish to ride horses trained by someone else. You may choose to only ride horses you have trained, or you may decide to train and let others ride. You may want to assist or oversee the work of others.

The nine secrets will help you find the very best within yourself, and free your creative potential to take you to your perfection.

In the physical training of a horse, the actions you take are yours. The actions taken by others are theirs. Understood or misinterpreted, those actions are exactly right for the time and place and the person. To tell you, or anyone else, that this is right and that is wrong, or that you must do "this" or you must do "that," would be imprudent on my part.

You have the creative potential. You posses infinite intelligence. You can be an innovator, an initiator, a follower of the heart.

The fact you have infinite intelligence and the creative potential to accomplish anything does not mean you will enjoy everlasting peace, perfect days and perfect nights. All will not be bliss. Blue sky, bright sunshine and smiling faces ever more is not your destiny. Your destiny is to experience everything so that you will in fact recognize perfection.

To know joy, you must know sadness; to know winning, there must be losing. Peace is only possible if you know chaos and relief only comes after the pain.

Accepting your creative potential and following your heart will change your life by changing the way you view and assess events. You will experience life just as you do now; however, you will not react to events as you do now.

For example, when training a horse, you may think your actions are correct, but they may not be the actions most desirable for the education of the horse. How do you react? Today you may become angry, thinking things have gone wrong. But if you accept your creative potential, you will come to understand that what seems an incorrect action is correct if it leads you to discover the proper action.

Are actions ever right or wrong? At the moment of the event, we give it label, a name, a viewpoint.

No matter the label, every event, every action is a learning experience for you, even events labeled "errors". If you study the experience as simply a message, learning comes more easily. If you ignore the message or fight it, you learn nothing and diminish the flow of your creative potential.

Every event, every action, also has a message for the horse. He will study it and learn from it, and what he learns, he will not easily forget.

If the horse learned the wrong thing from your action, it was still exactly correct, considering your experience and your intentions at the time. You will understand and be able to recognize eventually that the horse was required to learn the wrong thing so you could learn the right thing. When you are inexperienced at training or riding horses, doing a lot of the wrong things is actually the only way to move toward doing a majority of things right. Mistakes are a part of the learning process.

From the horse's viewpoint, however, there are physical reasons to avoid doing certain things wrong. It is in this area I may be of help to you and your horse.

The rule and guidelines I set out are basic to all trainers, to all styles of training and riding. The rule and guidelines are known to all who make a study of horsemanship. They are not exclusive to any system of training, nor to any breed of horse, nor to any endeavor of equestrian performance.

The rule is universal and adopted by all horsemen.

The rule is this: NEVER KNOWINGLY PLACE UNNECESSARY STRESS ON THE MUSCLE, SKELETAL OR NERVOUS SYSTEMS OF THE HORSE.

The key word here is "unnecessary."

Stress (forces pushing to limits) must be placed on the muscles or they will not grow stronger, more supple, capable of giving a superior performance. Stress must be placed on the skeletal system or the bones will not remodel, increasing density where needed as a prevention to injury. Stress must be placed on the nervous system, or the horse will not be calm in any circumstance, able to concentrate on the requests of the rider and thus move without distraction toward perfection.

Necessary stresses must be placed on the horse to bring him to a level of physical capability beyond that required to simply perform a specific action. The horse must be physically developed to such a point he can compete at a level of perfection, and yet be "well within himself." The horse must be stressed under controlled conditions. This means bones, muscle and mind must be worked to the point of being tired, but never exhausted. Every facet of the horse's being must be pushed and stretched by physical activity and the demand for concentration. He must be stressed over a period of time, and once the horse reaches an optimum level, he should be able to give a superior performance without damaging the muscles, bones or mind. He now must be held at that level for as long as possible by planned, short-term beneficial stresses.

Necessary stresses are an integral part of any training program. The ability of the trainer to design, implement and assess those stresses grows with increased knowledge and experience.

You must intentionally, not carelessly, stress the horse in order to improve your ability to train and/or ride the horse.

Even though the stresses may not always be well-designed or well-implemented, they will never be damaging if they are done with the best interest of the horse in mind. If you are training from the heart, you will never go wrong.

However, if you are training from the ego, demanding control over the horse instead of a partnership, the stresses will almost always be unnecessary. Such stresses are usually the result of the trainer/rider's attempt to appear dominate in

Chapter three

the eyes of others.

Reflect on it. Think about a time when you lost your temper and struck out at the horse. Weren't you trying to make something happen or make the horse behave in a certain way?

You may not have injured your horse. You may not even have stressed him unnecessarily, but under ego-directed circumstances, injuries happen.

My worst displays of temper, my worst losses of control have always come as a result of the frustration and anger I felt when things didn't go as I planned or wanted. My ego's desire for the approval of others, or my desire to control the horse, dragged me down to my lowest level as a horse trainer. When my ego took control, I lost, and so did the horse.

If you think first of the horse and what is best for him, your ego will be blocked, and you will never put unnecessary strain on the horse's physical and mental systems.

Much easier advised than practiced.

The difference between an ego-directed loss of control, which results in damaging punishment to a horse, and the planned, calculated discipline of a horse must be understood.

When you are guided by your ego, you lose your temper, are cruel and inhumane. You are out of control and inflict pain and physical and mental injury to your horse. When you examine your actions later under cooler conditions, they will always appear unnecessary and stupid.

Can your ego take the criticism of how you

treated your horse? It can, if you are maturing and gaining control of yourself. If it cannot take the truth, you have lost self-control and are ruled by your ego.

The standard by which you always judge your actions is: was the action truly in the best interest of the horse? If the answer is an honest "no," then your action was ego-directed.

If the answer is an honest "yes," then the action was from the heart, and was correct.

It is sometimes hard to understand how a particular physical discipline can be directed by your heart, and still be in the best interest of the horse. Consider this: a mare disciplines her foal with a physical punishment when she wishes to stop the foal's inappropriate behavior. She does so immediately, knowing she has centered the foal's attention on the unwanted behavior by giving a swift physical consequence. The pain from her kick or bite may be slight or fairly hard, but is effective if the behavior ceases. If the foal continues to misbehave after the initial reprimand, the foal will surely receive a stronger punishment. Increased punishment follows, until the foal grasps the message and learns a lesson: punishment of some kind is brought on by undesirable behavior. Cessation of such behavior is rewarded by ending the punishment.

The kick or bite is the punishment inflicted by the mare, and it is her form of discipline. Her discipline is given in the best interest of the foal. Well- behaved foals live longer.

A slap with a rope, a jerk on a shank or rein,

a thump of a heel, are forms of mild disciplines which a trainer or rider may use to discourage unwanted behavior. The discipline must come quickly, and it must be strong enough to get the horse's full attention.

If the horse is in the process of learning a particular behavior, then the discipline should be mild and brief, followed by an attempt to teach the desired behavior.

If the horse knows the correct response to a request, but simply refuses to comply, then the discipline must come quickly and should sting.

In either case, the discipline should be controlled and of such a nature as to correct the undesirable behavior. If it is, then it is from the trainer's heart, since it is done to improve the horse immediately, and to insure an easier, more pleasant and safe future.

If the handler's action is wild and meant to hurt the horse, then it is not discipline, but a tragic display of poor horsemanship.

I have been guilty of such displays, and they are not good for man nor horse. They are ego-directed, which makes them the most disgusting of actions. They severely damage the relationship between horse and trainer/rider, and they move the team away from the goal.

Yet every trainer, every rider, will experience such displays of temper and lack of control at one time or another. It is normal for humans. When ego prevails. Such behavior offers lessons. Learn from them.

Every horseman must work through the suppression of ego and conquer it by surrendering to his own heart. Only when the horseman follows his heart will he or she always act in the best interest of the horse, providing praise or discipline at the appropriate times.

Understanding the rule of not applying unnecessary stresses on the horse, as well as the concept of discipline, gives the horseman a solid foundation for training and riding--a foundation which has stood the test of time.

A horse always seeks comfort, or the avoidance of discomfort. Praise is comfortable. Horses naturally seek to avoid the discomfort of mild disciplines.

So called "affection" training and the use of gimmicks to avoid the responsibilities of discipline and horsemanship are the products of someone's ego seeking quick peer approval. Avoiding responsibility is not an action which comes from the heart. The heart is brave and accepts both the difficult and the easy.

When you read or hear of "progressive thinking" or new concepts in horse training, ask yourself: If this new method is used, is the trainer/rider giving of himself to make a permanent improvement in the horse? Or is the trainer/rider simply avoiding the responsibility of providing discipline? If the trainer is truly giving to make the horse better, rather than forfeiting his responsibility, then the concept is acceptable.

Understanding, then accepting the only rule

57

Chapter three

will help you to attain perfect horsemanship.

There are three guides to help you in your quest to abide by the rule. Each guide is a catalyst to a way of thinking.

The FIRST GUIDE is SLOW.

A plan of training based on slow but steady progress achieves rapid results. Slow movements around a horse provide for speedy trust. The slow, accurate, sensitive cueing of a horse brings immediate response.

There is nothing you can do quickly that isn't better done slowly.

Even the winning of a horse race, which is based primarily on the ability to move across a designated distance in the shortest possible time, most often goes to the "slow" horse. The horse with the greatest acceleration rate seldom wins the race at any distance. The greatest acceleration rate is invariably connected to the greatest deceleration rate, and when the two are combined over a distance, provide a greater elapsed time.

The horse with the slower acceleration generally reaches a greater speed and maintains it longer.

It's a fact. The "slow" horse is most often the fastest horse.

By taking the slow approach to training, riding and all forms of competition, short-term goals will be reached more quickly because the delays caused by wrong actions are lessened. If short-term goals are reached more quickly, then distant dreams move closer to realization.

Rushing the training of a performance horse brings on injury, both physical and mental. While physical injuries always take time to heal, the horse sometimes never recovers from the mental injury.

The use of drugs to speed recovery from injury so that performance can continue (even though healing is not complete) usually results in long-term delays.

Rushing anything you do with horses slows the arrival of the desired goal.

Slow is fast. Fast is a disaster.

The SECOND GUIDE to help you reach perfection in horsemanship is LOW.

Take the low approach to your training and riding and you will always be directing attention away from yourself and toward your horse. If you take the opposite "high" approach, you will be following the bidding of your ego, shouting, "Look at me. Like me."

Directing attention, especially your own, toward your horse gives you a low profile and the horse a high profile. He also gets the benefit of your concentrated assistance. Horses with high profiles win, and rider/trainers who are humble and quiet gain favor with everyone, even their competitors.

A quiet trainer uses a low voice, and low is the best voice to attract attention. It is said if you want someone to listen, whisper. It works with horses too.

Keep your voice low and calm, and your horse will soon be more attentive to you, waiting to hear that soothing request for work or the appreciated gentle praise. When you are working with a very inexperienced or young horse, your verbal communication should be crisp and given with the tone of authority. As the horse learns, the verbal communication should become more and more subtle. Finally, there will be no need for verbal commands, but plenty of opportunity for words of encouragement and praise that are low in volume.

Set low goals rather than lofty ones, and everything you do will succeed.

Setting low goals does not mean you think less of yourself or your horse. You know you and your horse have infinite ability. Still, you deliberately set low goals, not to avoid risk or challenge, but to assure there will always be success, and therefore, confidence for your horse. When you are training a green jumper, you begin by walking over ground poles, advancing to Cavalletis, and finally to very low jumps. If that is a natural progression, why shouldn't the same approach be taken when you seek a national championship?

Set low goals and succeed time after time after time. Nothing succeeds like success--winning brings winning and perfection brings perfection and perfect horsemanship is then close at hand.

Think low and speak low and reach the stars.

Conduct yourself as if you were below your horse, your horse's servant, if you will, and you will always conduct yourself well.

The THIRD GUIDE is NO CRITICISM.

Begin with no criticism of yourself. That does not mean you refuse to recognize your errors or your ego-directed behavior. It means you accept such behavior as a message for learning and a way of applying the secrets.

No criticism means no criticism of your horse.

Failure on your horse's part to interpret a cue correctly or to complete a request is not to be viewed as a loss or a problem, and should not be criticized. Instead, it should always be viewed as an opportunity to show the horse again just what it is you expect.

You may train a horse for years, win acclaim and awards, and still never achieve a totally flawless response to a series of cues. It is true with all horses and always will be. No horse will perform consistently without error. It is precisely for this reason that training goes on and on and on, even with the greatest of horses. Every mistake is there for a reason, and you can find an equal positive in every negative.

Instead of becoming frustrated at the misinterpretation of a cue, accept the horse's mistake--or your own--as a chance to improve the horse and yourself. It becomes a chance to give something of yourself to your partner. An error can be a chance for you to learn--a chance for you to refine your cue techniques and a chance to experiment with new ways to make training more interesting to the horse. Training is, after all, nothing more than the establishment of a system of communication between horse and rider.

No criticism also means no clash with the rules of the event in which you participate. If you believe a rule needs to be changed, work to change it. You will gain by taking the time and putting forth the effort. Horses, competitors and competitions all may benefit by the changing of rules or procedures. If in your heart you feel there is a better way, don't criticize, improve.

No criticism means not making disparaging remarks about competitors, trainers, horses or judges.

If you see nothing good in other trainers, riders or their horses, that is your loss and never theirs.

Everyone has a special talent. Search for it and learn from it, even if you never wish to adopt it.

To criticize others is to degrade yourself and use your energy in a wasteful and unproductive way.

Each time you want to criticize, stop and change the thought to a search for something which benefits you and your horse. Each time you do criticize, review the circumstances and discover the role your ego played. When you understand just how your ego wanted to control the situation or how your ego was seeking approval, you'll be able to stop your destructive thought and substitute constructive ideas.

No criticism means you will never weaken your relationship with your horse, but instead, will always be strengthening the bond.

At the beginning of this chapter I said it would be imprudent of me to tell you there was a right way or a wrong way to train horses. That statement is just one of the forms in which the third secret is expressed.

THIRD SECRET: PRACTICE NON-JUDGMENT.

It is not for you to judge whether any thought or action is wrong or right, is good or bad, is joyous or sad. Every event in your life will produce emotions. You will feel the emotions within your heart. The emotion should be recognized, experienced and accepted, but not judged. Each thing simply "is." You must try to see it as that and nothing more.

You have the power within you to change your ideas and desires into reality. You can make anything and everything happen when you allow your creative potential to act for you.

But your creative potential cannot easily create your desire if it is continually being blocked, weakened and misdirected by your ego. And your ego weakens and misdirects you every time you let it judge people and events.

Your ego is tiny, ineffective and ignorant, only a microsecond in forever when compared to the creative potential within you. The energy within you is infinite intelligence and the source of all things, and only it can know what truly "is."

Your ego makes judgments and these are always wrong because your ego is just too incompetent to see beyond the universe and understand beyond understanding. To be correct, you must accept everything as it is, without judgment.

Everything is "correct" even if you don't see the rightness of it. The fact that everything is correct

63

is a concept your ego cannot grasp.

Block your ego, surrender to your creative potential. Make no judgments. Accept events for the emotions felt and the lessons to be learned.

How other trainers train and how other riders ride are mirrors for you to see into yourself. Don't judge them; learn from them.

Follow the guide and move slowly, and you will have more time to reflect on events and more time to refuse to make a judgment.

Make no judgment and you won't speak or act too quickly. It has been said it is better to not speak and be thought a fool, than to speak and confirm the fact.

Follow the guide and choose to think "low" and you won't be thinking of yourself as so important that judgments are needed.

If you have creative potential and all others have the same creative potential, then you are not better nor worse than anyone else.

Your opinion is not better, your ideas are not better, your choices are not better. So why make a judgment about what others do, or say, or believe?

You should not.

The guide of making no criticism is the secret to the secret of non-judgment.

Make no judgments. View everything as simply an event from which to learn, the source of emotions to be experienced, a moment in the process of moving toward your perfection.

Chapter four
Giving is a perfect act

You have the power within you, and if you follow your heart, you can achieve anything you dare to dream.

Practice non-judgment. See everything for what it is--an event. Label it neither right nor wrong, but know it is perfect for the moment.

In every moment, try to find a way to give.

Every horse is unique, yet the same.

Every equestrian exercise is unique, yet the same.

Every sound horse is capable of performing any equestrian exercise. It is the individual horse's unique abilities which create the differences in levels of achievement.

It is the sameness in each horse and each exercise which becomes the foundation for the building of perfection.

Every horse needs to be well-schooled in the basics before refinements can be taught.

Chapter four

The essentials of an exercise must be mastered before the artistic expression can be added.

The proper development and education of a young horse creates the opportunity for the horse to achieve his ultimate performance.

Whether a particular horse does or does not reach projected goals will depend on his talent, his opportunities and the ability of his trainer to correctly identify the horse's potential.

The trainer must be extremely careful in his assessment of a horse's talents, recognizing what is common and what is special.

The trainer must see the potential of the horse's abilities, avoiding labeled judgments. This horse is a good horse, this horse is bad, this horse can, this horse cannot. Any horse's true value lies beyond such labels.

The trainer should evaluate the horse's physical and mental potential as expressed by the horse's natural inclinations. Those evaluations are the guides to the direction which should be taken to aid the horse's development.

Whatever the horse's unique talent, it is that ability which should be cultivated. You are seeking talent suited to an intention, and you must maintain and focus your attention on the talent and the goal. Do not focus on the horse's training, attempting to force a horse to perform in contradiction to his natural abilities.

Recognizing a horse's talent includes knowing when the horse's abilities lie in areas other than your intended goals. If the horse's talent is not suited to the trainer's intentions, then the horse should be removed from that program and placed elsewhere.

The horse's owner must also recognize the horse's talent and then be brave enough to allow the horse to develop in that direction.

There is no compromise.

If you want a particular horse so much you are willing to change your desires, great. But if you are not willing or knowledgeable enough to accept the horse for what he is, you will fail to reach your potential and so will the horse.

If the horse cannot be what you want, let him reach his potential and perfection in someone else's hands.

Releasing the horse from enforced restraints, creating freedom, is the essence of the FOURTH SECRET: GIVE!

Give the horse every opportunity to reach his full potential and you will reach yours.

Give the horse every opportunity to be a champion and you will become a champion.

Give the horse your very best and you will be better than you ever dreamed possible.

If you want to reach perfection with performance horses, if you want to win competitions, you must place the horse in an event for which he has true and natural talent. You must "give" him the chance. Anything less results in less.

There is no question any horse can be trained to perform any exercise you choose. But without

Chapter four

equal or greater specific talent, no horse can out-perform well-trained horses naturally gifted for a particular sport. Asking a horse to perform above his level or in a competition for which he is not suited is "taking" from the horse, not "giving." To take from the horse is to take from yourself. If you persist, you will take so much from the horse he will soon have no desire, no opportunity, no time left to reach his potential. And your time and your effort will also be gone, unrewarded.

You reap only what you sow. Give!

Time is easy to lose and hard to find. Give your time, rather than taking the horse's, and you will find plenty of time to be everything you desire.

Like every horse, every person has a special talent. Find your special training or riding talent and apply it to the special talent of your horse. Perfection is then guaranteed.

The search for a horse's ability begins with the horse's breeding.

I have already acknowledged any breed of horse can, to some degree, perform any event. But the best horses bred for a particular event will win the highest awards for that competition. It's a fact. Ignoring the inherent potential and talents of specific breeds of horses only results in frustration and loss.

When selecting a horse, don't decide on a particular breed, then try to find evidence to support your intentions. Rather, learn the facts. Know which breed of horse most often triumphs in the event in which you expect to excel. Go with the facts. Give the horse you select every chance to be a

68

winner rather than face an impossible struggle.

To reach perfection with performance horses, you must experience that moment when both you and the horse are giving fully of your greatest talents.

To win and reach perfection, you must work with a horse which has the natural ability necessary to excel in your chosen event. A horse with no jumping ability, even if he tries, cannot reach perfection, and he cannot win the competition. A horse which has no "cow" can go through the motions of being a cutting horse, but he cannot reach his own perfection, nor can he win. Any horse can perform as a dressage horse, but without the natural talents, he can never deliver the powerful performance required to reach the highest standards.

To reach perfection in any competition, a horse must be given freedom, letting his natural talents carry him to his potential.

It is that simple. To make it more complicated is only an exercise in futility and frustration.

If you are breeding your potential champion, you may have the opportunity to imprint the new born. Imprinting involves the thorough handling of the foal within hours of birth, conditioning the foal to be touched and restrained by man.

Imprinting certainly makes life easier in many ways for both the young horse and handler, but it is not essential. If your horse was not imprinted at birth, he will be instructed in proper behavior as his early training progresses.

Chapter four

Remember, when working with any horse, discipline is required. Loss of temper or patience are to be avoided.

With young horses, never plan on a training session of more than a few minutes. You can work with the young horse five, six, seven or more times a day, but limit each session to 10 minutes or less.

Training sessions for older horses should not be too long. Always keep in mind the horse has limited ability to concentrate. Teach the lesson, the communication, then give the horse time to absorb the new information.

The first lesson every horse--foal or older--must learn is to respect restraint, in other words, hold still.

With a foal, you can simply put an arm under his neck and grab his tail with the other hand. If the foal is especially rowdy, grab the tail with one hand and place the other arm over the foal's neck so you can use your body to push the neck down and prevent rearing and/or head tossing. With just a few practice sessions, the foal will learn to let himself be caught and gently restrained. Soon, he'll stand relatively still. You can then teach the foal to let you touch him all over, and lift his feet.

Older horses too must learn to stand still. Verbal commands, gentle tugs on the lead, and plenty of practice will usually do the trick. Don't hesitate, however, to use a chain over the nose or a lip chain on stubborn horses.

Learning to stand still is a must for the horse. There are many good books on the breaking and training of horses. If you are just beginning, or it is necessary for your horse to be reschooled, I suggest you read, discuss, and take advice from those who have plenty of experience in the initial training of young horses. From your research, study and personal experience, you can then formulate a plan for the basic training or reschooling of your horse. Finally, before starting, improve the plan by discarding any suggestions for force, shortcuts or the use of specialized equipment.

Horses which reach perfection at any age are given ample time to learn their lessons. They are never forced into any response, and they need no gimmicks in order to learn. It should be noted now that the best trainers and the best horses in any and every event, with few exceptions, use the mildest snaffles or curb bits. For the most part, training equipment is kept to protection devices to eliminate cuts, scrapes or bruises.

However, if training is transferred from acceptable cues and aids to the force of external apparatus, the horse is essentially lost, as the secret of "giving" is ignored and everything becomes "taking."

Before you begin any training which involves the movement of a horse, you must accept this fact: all action initiates in the hindquarters.

ALL ACTION INITIATES IN THE HINDQUARTERS is the FIRST ELEMENT of horse training.

Within this element there is an answer to all questions regarding the performance of a horse.

Chapter four

You can only understand the movement of the horse, from walk to Capriole, from gallop to jump, from sliding stop to haunches out, when you know where the action initiates.

To move forward, the horse contracts and extends the muscles of the hindquarters to push the body out of balance. From the action of the hindquarters, the horse loses his balance forward, then immediately extends his front legs forward to catch himself and reestablish equilibrium.

The principle is the same whether he is moving forward, backward or laterally.

All action initiates in the hindquarters.

The proof of this truth is seen in the horse's conformation. His rear legs are designed for driving. His hind feet are shaped and cupped to grip the ground as his entire hindquarters propel the body. The front feet and legs are designed specifically to catch a moving body. The front feet are round, making a solid base upon which a front leg can be locked into a stationary position. The front leg is a column of bones held in position by tendons and ligaments so a forward moving mass can be supported. There is no conformational suggestion that the forehand of the horse provides any type of propulsion. In fact, the front foot is retracted just after reaching its farthest extension so it may be strategically placed under an already moving mass.

It is because all action initiates in the hindquarters that a rider never pulls on a horse to stop or turn. It is because all action initiates in the hindquarters that all control over the horse is exercised through the hindquarters.

The horse's mouth, head or forehand cannot provide the rider with a means for control over the horse's body.   No matter how much force is applied to the mouth, head or forehand, horses still run away, fall or flip over.   Forehand control is not horse control.

The mouth, the head and the forehand are areas for communication.

Speak to the horse through the forehand. Initiate power action through the hindquarters.

Understanding the principle that all action initiates in the hindquarters is not a secret of perfection with performance horses.   It is one of the basic and required elements for the training of any horse for any performance.

Performance horses which win, which reach perfection, are horses which are so well-schooled in the basics they can accept and dismiss any type of external distraction.   They can adjust instantly to changing situations and cues, and they can be relied upon to respond, if not perfectly, at least adequately every time to the two foundation commands--(1) stop; (2) stand quietly, yet attentively.

The two behaviors just described are way beyond the ability of the average performance horse. That may seem ludicrous to say, but it is true, and is demonstrated by the fact so few performance horses ever achieve winning records.

Such solid basic behavior is seldom, if ever, seen in the average horse.

This is so because few horsemen require or

expect the horse to stop all action and then stand quietly, yet attentively. Any behavior approximating these goals seems to satisfy most trainers/riders.

"Ho," or "Stop" is the first lesson the performance horse must learn. "Ho" does not mean the horse should slowly come to a halt or slow his forward progress. It does not mean he should be generally cooperative and a relatively likable guy.

"Ho" means stop....do not move...cease all action immediately.

When the command, "Ho", is given verbally or in conjunction with a physical cue, the horse must respond instantly and without hesitation.

Before any further performance training is started, "Ho" must be mastered--not for the moment, but for all time.

You can teach the "Ho" on the lead line by using the verbal command, followed by a sharp jerk on the lead. The young horse, after several demonstration jerks, should pick up the idea of stopping forward action. This is not a difficult lesson, but one which requires gentle, persistent reinforcement.

Once the horse masters the "Ho," the handler must never say "Ho" when he or she means something else. "Ho" should mean the same for the trainer/rider as it does for the horse--stop all action instantly. Confusing the horse by using an unintentional "Ho" leaves the horse uncertain about any command or cue. If the very first command does not mean the same thing every time, how can the horse be expected to determine what any cue means at a particular time?

Be consistent. Say what you mean when communicating with your partner. And mean what you say!

When the horse knows the command and cue to stop while on the lead line and the horse is old enough, advance the lesson to the longe line.

Give the horse time to recognize a verbal or physical cue. Give him time to evaluate. Give him time to respond and give him time to think about his actions.

Learning to use a longe line is important and relatively easy. Most good trainers can teach you the refinements once you have perfected the basics.

The longe line is a useful tool for providing exercise for the horse. But during this exercise, the establishment of you as the one requesting action and the horse as the one responding (the primary use of the longe line) must be the first thought in the handler's mind. While many good lessons can be practiced on the longe line, all are wasted or diminished if the horse is allowed to perform any movement other than what is requested.

Teach the horse to walk, trot, canter and stop on verbal command. Teach the horse to use his entire body while working on the longe.

There are two helpful rules to follow when working a horse on the longe line. First, always keep your body behind the horse's natural balance point when asking the horse to move forward, but move your body to a position forward of the natural balance point if you wish the horse to stop forward action.

Second, always move toward the horse to engage action. Move toward the horse, driving him away to enlarge the circle, and move toward the horse while shortening the line to decrease the circle. Never back away from the horse.

Keeping these rules in mind will help you maintain your system of communication with the horse, as well as initiate the correct action from the horse's hindquarters.

Training techniques on the longe line include everything from free exercise to work while the horse is tacked or bit up in a show frame.

How much or how little work you want to do with the longe line is up to you. It is a useful tool, and I like it when starting babies.

I teach young horses to walk, trot, canter and stop on the longe line after they have reached eight or nine months of age. The lessons are short and require so little work the youngsters never break a sweat.

A friend once told me, "Never get a young horse hot and you'll never have a bad training session." I believe he was right, and I believe it to be a part of the secret of "giving." Ending the work session with a brief rest and a kind word of praise is giving your horse a gift, or reward for a job well-done.

By the time the horse has reached the age of 14 months, he has had plenty of romp and stomp time with others of his own age and has been conditioned on the longe line. It is now time to teach him to carry a rider.

Thousands, nay millions, will protest loudly that the horse is too young to be ridden. They will say he is not yet strong enough and he has not stopped growing. His knees aren't closed yet.

Every protester will have at least two more reasons you should never ride such a young horse, and every protester will cry out, "That barbarian should by lynched."

Sorry, but I ignore it all.

Give, don't take!

Give him the greatest gift you can. Give him an education which will protect him from abuse and mishandling all his life.

Give him a strong body conditioned to work without stress.

Give him suppleness, sharp reflexes and sinew.

Start him early so his body can develop correctly, so his bone will be strong and his mind will be calm.

If you start him when he is young, you can give him plenty of time. There is no rush to catch up if you are always ahead.

Give the young horse your best training, unhurried, carefully planned, in short sessions, never demanding instant results.

I take no less than one month to introduce the young horse to the saddle, the bridle and the rider.

Each day I longe the youngster, with plenty of rest stops, for up to 10 minutes. At the end of the

Chapter four

longeing session, I show the horse the saddle cloth,
the saddle and the bridle. I may lay them on his
back, rub them against his neck, even place the bit
in his mouth. When he is quite content, the training
session is over.

Progress is rapid because we go slowly.

Usually within a week the youngster can be
completely groomed, saddled and bridled without
incident.

I never want the young horse to buck, rear or
throw a fit about the placement of equipment. Such
behavior is avoided by not forcing the issue. The
horse can have all the time needed. This does not
mean there is no discipline. If a student does not
behave properly, there is an appropriate reprimand
to get his attention back on the subject.

Once the horse accepts being tacked, he is
walked in his stall for several minutes. As soon as
he is completely comfortable being tacked, he can be
longed that way. Never allow the tacked horse to
buck while being longed. If he should attempt such
behavior, control the situation by stopping all action.
Let the horse settle, then restart him at the walk.

Don't hurry. The tiniest step toward progress
today becomes a giant leap forward tomorrow.

After being longed with tack, I take the horse
to his stall and introduce him to weight in the
stirrup. Several days of slapping the saddle,
popping the leathers and putting a foot in the stirrup
is usually all it takes to thoroughly convince even
the most skittish youngster there is no danger.

I step up on the young horse when he shows

he hasn't a care in the world. I stay in the saddle only a moment or two, then step down. Work from both sides. Get up on the left, off on the right, then vice versa.

Do not change the training sequence. Add something new to something old. Always proceed in that manner.

The daily routine is the same, with something new added at the end. The introduction of new information should be brief, extending the training session for only a few minutes. To keep the training sessions from getting too long (more than 20 minutes) reduce the time spent with the most familiar routine.

As soon as the youngster accepts my presence in the saddle as a normal occurrence, I begin to work the bit. A light tug is given on one rein until the horse moves his nose in the direction of the tug. Never pull and maintain the pressure on the rein. The proper action is a tug and an immediate release. You must give the horse his freedom. When he is free and responds by turning his head after the tug cue, praise him, and work in the opposite direction. The lesson should last only a matter of minutes.

Within days, the horse will respond to the lightest of tugs. He will be willing to turn his nose to your leg. In fact, he will often do it on his own just to see what's there.

The basis for a light mouth has been established.

Now you can begin to walk the horse in the stall. Use the verbal command followed by a light tap of your heel and a light tug on the rein. In giving the tug on the rein and by responding to the verbal command, the horse will lose his balance forward and take a step to regain his equilibrium. He is walking. The horse is broke to ride, and absolutely nothing dramatic has happened.

Walk in circles, stopping and changing direction. The time spent riding in the stall depends on the horse and your confidence. Stay in the stall walking, stopping and turning until there is no doubt in your mind the horse will respond instantly to your turning and stopping cues.

When you are ready, have someone open the stall door and walk the horse out. Walk around the barn, or corral, or pasture. Walk, turn and stop.

Give the horse his full 30 days before even thinking of adding something new. He has learned quite enough.

Short progressive lessons, together with the gift of time, are the blueprints for the training or reschooling of any horse, at any age and at any level.

You have given the horse respect and understanding. In return, you will get his.

You have given the horse some of your talent.

You will be reward by knowing his talent.

But more than anything, you have given the horse a basis for a happy, healthy, productive future.

Upon that foundation, he'll give you everything.

Chapter five
Choose to know the truth

Why study horses and horsemanship?
To gain knowledge and improve yourself?
No!
Study horses and horsemanship to know the truth so your learning will benefit the horse.

Knowledge is the knowing, or understanding, of the information you have about a subject.

A little knowledge actually means there is a lot more to know, and the discovery of new information is what makes learning interesting. The more interesting a subject becomes, the more we try to learn. Yet learning is never complete. Each time we learn something, we empower ourselves to gain much more knowledge.

Knowledge is always incomplete, and being incomplete, then frequently not the truth.

Example: a horseman, thought by many to be knowledgeable, may define a snaffle bit as "a bit with a jointed mouthpiece."

That is knowledge which is incomplete and therefore not the truth.

A snaffle MAY have a jointed mouthpiece. A bit is a snaffle only when it has no poll action, no curb action, and the reins attach to the cheek piece directly opposite whatever the mouthpiece.

More knowledge had to be added to make the offered response truth.

You've heard, "Pull back on the reins to stop a horse."

Knowledgeable horsemen have said it, but it is false.

Pulling back on the reins to make a horse stop would seem the most appropriate thing to do, but it is advice based on common practice and incomplete knowledge. (We'll examine stopping cues and the horse's physical response later in this chapter.)

Acceptance of widespread information is a conditioned response. Acceptance does not make it correct. You must make an effort to gain complete knowledge to know the truth.

Learning is a joy, a delight, a process of letting your infinite intelligence guide you to your destiny. But don't study just to gain knowledge. Study to increase your ability to give to others.

Giving is the greatest expression of wisdom.

Study and learn so your knowledge is complete enough to be truth.

Find the truth for the benefit of your horses and your students.

Choose your responses

When you think of horses and horsemanship, the amount to be known may seem overwhelming.

It is not.

It is endless.

But well within your capacity.

The more you study, the more you realize how little you know, and the greater the amount there is to be learned. At the same time, you will understand the more you know, the less you need to express your knowledge in intellectual terms. You will begin to feel more and think less.

When you know a great deal about horses, you will know there is much more to learn, but it is only interesting, not necessary. It polishes, but the foundation is unchanged.

After you have learned a great deal about training horses, you will know there are only six basic elements which apply to any and all performance horses.

Beyond the six elements of training, there is nothing.

But it is in the nothingness that the artist, the poet, the innovator begins to work his or her magic.

It is only in the nothingness that the training and riding transcend the physical and become thought, and the SECRETS are applied and the perfection begins.

Master the six elements so your knowledge is the truth.

When you know the truth, you will be confident in your actions.

The six elements of training, in sequence of

Chapter five

understanding and application, are:

1. ALL ACTION INITIATES IN THE HORSE'S HINDQUARTERS.
2. COMMUNICATION: REQUESTS AND RESPONSES.
3. COMPLIANCE THROUGH NONRESISTANCE.
4. IMPULSION: POWER IN MOVEMENT.
5. SUPPLENESS: THE REQUIREMENT FOR GRACE IN ACTION.
6. COLLECTION: CONTROLLING THE BALANCE POINT.

The first element, that "all action initiates in the hindquarters" was introduced in Chapter Four. It will be discussed often as more of the secrets of perfect horsemanship are revealed.

COMMUNICATION, the second element, is offered with the understanding that the action to follow will begin in the horse's hindquarters.

Communication begins with the most simple, emphatic cues to elicit the most simple of responses. It evolves until it can be lavish praise for work well-done, or a gentle pat on the neck for a good effort. Communication can also be a punishment for failure to obey. Communication can be thought between partners.

Unfortunately, too often communication can be an undesirable conditioned response. A coach suggests a change in riding, and the student snaps back, "I like it this way." A conditioned response to a perceived criticism. A response defending the ego. A response without the thought of the secret of "giving."

Whatever it is, communication is actually all that a horse ever learns from a trainer.

Shortly after birth, the horse can perform all the maneuvers he will ever be asked for by a rider. The hours-old foal can run, jump, stop, spin, change leads on the fly and pivot. No human trains the horse to perform such actions.

Through observation and understanding we learn the horse's physical abilities. As trainers and riders, all we do is ask the horse to perform to our request that which he is already capable of doing.

Trainers simply teach communication and act as physical conditioning supervisors. That's it.

The communication system starts with the verbal communication "Ho" which is used with the foal as the first effort to have him hold still. The "Ho" communication is offered again and again as the teaching and the horse progress. The consistent use of the same cue, reinforced by reward and confrontation (a requirement of learning), eventually brings about the desired response. That is training. That is teaching a communication system.

Training is directed at soliciting the same response from each horse each time a rider gives a specific cue or sequence of cues.

Knowledge of horses is the foundation upon which you build your communication. The more complete knowledge you have of horses, the stronger the foundation of understanding. The more you understand how a horse thinks and moves, the better you will be able to choose the cues you use.

Horses are herd animals, herbivores. They are hunted by carnivores, so they think and act as prey. Humans are predators, thinking and acting as such.

Horses are constantly aware of all things around them so they can be ready to flee at the first sign of danger.

Man tends to focus exclusively on his goal at the time, ignoring external factors.

It is this basic difference between our natural inclinations which create the greatest problems in developing communication.

Trainers and riders must first seek to understand the horse, both mentally and physically, then attempt to communicate their desires.

Genuine communication is possible only through a knowledge of the horse's mental processes, which are, in order of importance: herd instinct, need for security, the following instinct, love of routine, laziness, excitability and nervousness, sensitivity and courage.

Horses are mentally consistent and reasonable, while much of the time their handlers are not. When trainers fail to consider the horse's mental processes, troubles begin, and then, all too often, handlers forget it's a matter of communication rather than physical control by force.

During the first efforts at communication, the voice, hands, body, seat, legs, heels and weight of the rider are most often used separately when asking for specific performance.

Novice riders and trainers are faced with the problem of having to think of each cue, then apply it. Using the hands, seat, legs and weight together and in harmony can be a monumental task for the beginner. But with hours and hours of practice, it becomes efficient and acceptable. Finally, with confidence born of competence, the result is graceful and worthy of praise.

But it never reaches perfection until communication transcends the physical and becomes effortless thought.

This happens when the rider is no longer centered on himself, but is a true partner of the horse. They are one. The rider thinks of the desired performance and no more. Thoughts become the cues without conscious direction. The horse responds to the mental cues and performs as a gift to his partner. Together horse and rider enter a "zone" or state of action awareness in which the two blend so naturally that sliding, spinning, jumping or racing are perfect and effortless, without conscious interference. The blend is creative potential realized. It is beyond thought.

Communication with the horse begins as a visual contact. The horse sees you and is happy or fearful. If the horse likes what he sees, he'll generally come to you for more communication. If he is fearful, getting to know each other may take some time.

On the ground, your visual positioning to the horse can block forward movement, or create it.

Verbal commands, "ho, walk, trot, canter," are

easily learned by the horse. He'll also respond, but not necessarily as desired, to screams of fear, shouts and swearing.

Verbal cues should always be clear and concise. When you speak to a horse be firm, but gentle.

Physical cues begin with hands. A light touch can be soothing; a slap can be punishment. In riding, the hands should be soft, but firm. The horse is always ridden into the hands. (All action initiates in the hindquarters, and then moves forward.) The hands never make a steady pull on the reins.

The hands and the reins control the start and stop of action and the direction of travel. The hands send a subtle signal through the reins by a slight movement of the reins. This tells the horse action is about to begin. The hands may shorten or lengthen the reins to establish the desired body length of the horse, telling the horse the desired gait. The horse's body is at its longest when walking, so a long rein is required. A shorter rein may signal a trot, while a still shorter rein calls for a canter.

Direct and indirect reins communicate the direction of travel and precisely where the horse's head and nose will be positioned.

The hands may give a tug on the reins to tip the nose of the horse being schooled into the desired direction, or the hands might give a more severe tug as a punishment to a young horse foolishly misbehaving.

In any and all cases, rein action is followed

immediately by no action. There is no constant rein pressure. When the horse moves into the hands and is "on the bit" there is contact through the reins.

There is never a steady pulling pressure on the reins, and the only acceptable constant rein contact occurs when the horse is "on the bit" due to impulsion, the moving forward.

The seat is used to create greater engagement of the horse's back and hindquarters.

A relaxed rider will be sitting down in the saddle, with straight back and hips. If the hips are dropped backward or pushed forward, new pressure will be applied to the horse's back. By tightening the stomach muscles, for example, the hips are driven backward, and the rider's weight is forced down and toward the back of the saddle. At the same time, the rider's upper body is held rigid by the tightening of the abdominal muscles. The upper body cannot be leaned forward or backward. This is the movement used by the rider to bring a horse to a quick stop, driving the horse's hindquarters forward, rounding the back upward and pushing the horse into the bit, which is held steady as a barrier to further progress.

The legs are used to communicate movement, following the initial information given to the horse through the hands and reins.

Pressure from the leg causes the horse to contract or extend muscles. If the rider applies right leg pressure and the horse's right hind foot is on the ground, the horse will extend the muscles on the right side and push himself forward. If the right hind foot is off the ground, the horse will contract the muscles, lifting the foot higher.

In early communication, a lot of the rider's leg surface is used to apply pressure. As performance skills improve, less pressure is required, and a more precise application is necessary. A rider's lower leg is wide, and a heel is about two inches across, so the leg and heel touch a relatively large area of the horse's side. To make cues more refined and precise, spurs are used. Spurs are not applied for punishment, but are used as instruments for very accurate pressure placement. The spur's accurate placement tells the horse which of his parts you are most interested in moving--back, middle or front.

In addition to guiding movement and the amount of effort desired, the legs aid in direction. The horse may be asked to move away from a leg or bend around it. The horse may be asked for more impulsion by the leg or for a change of foot flight pattern. With the well-schooled horse, leg contact is light and constant. The release of contact reports to the horse that something new is coming; be prepared.

A rider's weight is always present, so it always communicates, and it always assists or detracts from performance.

Positioning of the rider's weight directly affects the horse's ability to collect himself. In order to be in "collection", the horse must move his natural balance point from its position just behind and above the elbow to a position under the rider's weight. The horse can only move his balance point under the rider's weight by moving his hindquarters forward, thereby picking up more of his own forehand weight.

It is my opinion no rider--even a race rider--should have his or her basic weight forward of the horse's natural balance point. Having a rider's weight too far forward, which is seen regularly in jumping and race riding, makes it nearly impossible for the horse to use his back properly, resulting in a major loss of power. The rider who puts his weight forward causes the horse to use just his legs for movement, rather than utilizing his entire body.

Properly trained, a horse will attempt to move under the rider's shifting weight, thereby bringing the team back into balance. But he will also move away from shifting weight so lateral movement is possible. The horse will know which is desired based on the speed of the action required.

Only the western horse does a singularly lateral movement, the sidepass. In the sidepass to the right, the rider would shift his weight to the left, and the horse would move away from the weight shift. The same horse, however, would move toward the right, toward the weight shift, if the rider were asking for a rollback to the right. The sidepass is done slowly, while the rollback is negotiated with speed. The speed of the action is all the horse needs to signal his movement away from or toward a weight shift.

In early training, cues and communication are exaggerated for all horses and riders. As cue vocabulary increases, and understanding keeps pace, communication becomes more and more

91

refined.

Finally communication becomes thought, and even though the hands, seat, legs and weight do in fact signal the horse, there is no conscious direction of the action. The thought of a perfect performance transforms itself into reality. You will know the truth of this when you recognize it happens to you countless times each day. You walk, talk, run, skip and jump, and never know or analyze the mechanics. It is simply an effortless thought, and then a reality.

As you gain knowledge, and determine the truth of what you are learning, you can begin employing the FIFTH SECRET: MAKE CONSCIOUS CHOICES ABOUT HOW YOU RESPOND.

For example, if your first response to the question, "What is a snaffle?" was "A bit with a jointed mouthpiece," your answer was most likely based on what you had been told previously. Your reply was "conditioned" or shaped by that information, whether right or wrong. Your answer was not reasoned or determined.

The conditioned response is the result of a lack of self esteem and mental laziness which allows others to control your thinking. If heard frequently enough, the lazy mind accepts anything as truth.

Only someone self assured and seeking knowledge for the benefit of his horse will study bits and their uses, and learn the complete definitions and the correct uses of the equipment. Such a person will eventually experience moments of perfect horsemanship, for it is that person who will put forth the necessary effort to make conscious choices rather than conditioned replies.

Test the truth of all you think you know.

An example of a conditioned response is the belief that pulling back on the reins is the correct way to stop a horse. This method is advanced by trainers and riders and teachers who have not sought the truth of their knowledge, but have just accepted "input." They did not challenge the information they were given, and they never considered their horse in seeking the truth. They are conditioned responders, never giving, taking instead, always blocking their creative potential.

Challenge all information so you can make choices in your responses.

By understanding how a horse moves, and how a horse learns the communication system being taught, you will know a horse is stopped in early training by using the verbal command, "Ho." When riding a horse and asking for the stop, the horse is given information he understands--the verbal command, "Ho", followed by the rider tightening his stomach muscles to push his seat deep into the saddle, and squeezing with both legs to drive the horse's hindquarters forward. The last rider cue is the taking of the slack from the reins. This is not pulling back on the reins, merely taking the slack so that the bit now becomes a barrier to forward movement. Once the horse stops, the rider immediately releases his leg pressure and extends the rein.

The horse responds to the stopping cues by

preparing for the stop on the verbal command, rounding his back to accommodate the forward moving hindquarters, and lifting slightly and flexing at the poll to remain behind the bit barrier.

As training progresses, the verbal command is eliminated. Establishment of the bit barrier is more subtle, as are the other cues, and the horse comes to a relaxed square stop, or if in a different performance, slides to a stop. (The western slide stop differs from the square stop in that the rider does not use his or her legs to squeeze the horse into the bit barrier. Instead of squeezing the horse forward, the western rider removes leg pressure and stops riding the horse forward, letting the horse slide based on his momentum and inertia.)

In every case, the reins are not pulled back, rather the horse is driven forward to the bit barrier established by setting the hands.

Making the conscious choice to know the truth and the conscious effort to apply that truthful knowledge will be confirmed by the heart as the right thing to do if "giving" is involved in the response.

When you make a conscious choice to be sure "giving" is always a part of your response, good feelings result for you and those around you, particularly your horse.

As with stopping, the rider does not pull back on the reins in order to back his horse. That idea is a response perpetuated by misinformation which has not been challenged. As you know, all action begins in the hindquarters, so whether you are moving forward or backward, the correct action does not come from pressure on the horse's mouth.

Instead of pulling on the reins, the knowledgeable rider backs a horse properly by shortening the reins gently until the horse shifts the majority of his weight from the forehand to the hindquarters. There is no rein pulling action involved. The reins are simply shortened by the hands until the horse very quietly and almost imperceptibly shifts to the hindquarters. The rider must not change his weight or the length of the rein, but must then ask for movement by squeezing with both legs. The horse will move to the rear. He will continue to move rearward until the rider's leg pressure is removed. The horse will stop upon the release of the leg pressure, but will move rearward again if the rider has not changed the rein position and reapplies leg pressure. The horse will not move forward until the rider lengthens the rein, allowing the horse to shift his weight once again to the forehand. Leg pressure will then move the horse forward.

Rearward direction of travel is controlled by a combination of leg and rein pressure against the horse's neck. Rearward speed is controlled by the amount of leg pressure applied.

If the rein position is correct to get the horse to shift his weight to the hindquarters before asking for rearward movement, the horse will never toss his head, nor open his mouth to escape bit pressure, for there will be none.

Question information, no matter who is offering it. "Authority" must be challenged, not in a negative way, but in a search for the truth, which always includes giving.

Making conscious choices about how you respond to everything--means everything!

Example--a horse steps on your toe. What is your response?

I've been known to say naughty words, give the horse a thump or stinging lash with the lead rope, or just push him away and think, "Be more careful." Two bad responses, one good.

A response without giving is almost always action-filled or violent, for the conditioned response is almost always the ego response. The ego seeks the approval of others, or control over others. The slap and curse word are ego responses attempting to make the horse the villain and the handler the macho boss.

If you have been guilty of such actions, you know it was wrong for it did not bring happiness to you or those around you. You certainly weren't pleased with your response, and were probably a little embarrassed by your actions. Later, you felt even worse, at least that's the way it has been for me. I certainly didn't make myself or the horse happy. All the horse got was some pain, maybe a new fear and an unwanted communication.

Nothing positive results unless conscious choices which include "giving" are your decisions.

Whatever the event, the circumstances or the frustration, you need to slow down, take some time, draw upon your knowledge, and seek the truth. Then make a conscious choice as to how to respond to events.

Choices need not always be immediate. Take time to consider the event. Speed has nothing to do with the correctness of a choice.

Will your response to a less than perfect performance be a resolution to work harder? In some cases it should be, but in most cases it should not.

The incorrect response is often, "work harder," because that is the response of reason, the conditioned response, the response of the ego which strives to control everything. The response from the heart will be to "work smarter." You work smarter when you call upon your infinite intelligence to provide answers to the questions you ponder.

If you do not immediately find an answer satisfactory to your heart, you will have to seek new information until you discover the truth.

Your heart will tell you when you have found the truth, and your heart will guide you to the right action, even though the action may not make you happy at the moment. For example, the decision to seek a new horse may seem a sad one. But will the horse you are riding be happy if he simply doesn't have the physical capabilities or mental capacity to perform to your expectations?

Will you be happy with poor performances? Are you "giving" to a horse when the horse tries, but can't succeed?

Conscious choices without giving, the ones most commonly made, are always wrong, for they are not the responses of your creative potential.

Chapter five

They are responses of the ego.

I've probably made nearly all the wrong responses a trainer or rider can make over a long span of years. My ego made those choices, either to control the horse rather than give to him, or to win the approval of others at the expense of my horse. My heart did not make any of those wrong choices. None were based in truthful knowledge, and none provided positive communication to the horse.

I apologize for so many mistakes.

Fortunately for many horses, I learned the fifth secret from a friend who practices it to perfection.

Meribah can face any situation and without hesitation, fully conscious of her choice, make the correct decision. Her heart rules her choices and her choices always include giving.

She always chooses, not for her ego, but for others. I've never known her to lose her temper or her self-control. She is exceptional, which makes it the norm for those she touches to know the joy of her giving.

Chapter six
Everything is exactly right

The inevitable questions:

If my creative potential exists, and I have the power to accomplish anything, why do things go wrong?

If my intentions and desires are to be realized, why aren't they reality now?

To those watching from outside the ring, training the performance horse clearly seems the most wonderful way in the world to spend your time. Friends, neighbors, even strangers have told me, "You're so lucky, getting to work with horses all day."

Of course they're right. I am lucky. I'm fulfilling my potential, and my desires are becoming my reality.

I am doing the work I want to do.

But work was not what they were seeing. Their opinions sprang from a perception quite different from mine.

What they saw was a man riding a horse. To

them, riding is not work, but recreation, fun, an escape from the everyday world.

For so many, work is seen as unpleasant, filled with frustrations, difficulties and endless problems.

Work, if not your heart's desire, is stressful.

But in watching the horse and rider, the spectators saw no stress, no problems, no frustrations. They saw the beauty of a country setting, the blue sky, and a marvelous horse.

They saw a scene, and deemed training horses a pleasant, enjoyable experience. That was their perception, and for them it was the truth.

But horsemen know there can be other perceptions of the same scene and other realities.

Sometimes it is not all blue sky and marvelous horses. Sometimes it is hot, or cold, or dry or wet. It's one mistake after another, one difficulty after another, one problem on top of another. There are injuries to deal with, and sickness, and horses which simply don't have the talent to achieve the goals. There are a thousand big and little irritating things that go wrong. There are frustrations, if that is the way you choose to see it.

Whatever the perception, in reality it is no more, nor any less, than what exists for everyone, in every endeavor.

It is what it is. It is what you choose it to be.

It is also the SIXTH SECRET: EVERYTHING IS EXACTLY AS IT SHOULD BE.

Don't fight the moment.

There are no chance happenings.

Nothing is random.

From the smallest molecule to the largest galaxy, everything has a purpose, a direction, a function. Everything is of equal importance to every other thing, and while all things are different, they are always interdependent.

Everyone and everything carries the same creative potential. Everyone and everything has a purpose and a function. No matter what the purpose or function is labeled, no purpose, no function is greater nor less than any other.

Nothing you are doing is by accident. All of what you are and what you are doing is the result of your choices. You are where you are supposed to be at this moment.

So if everything is exactly as it should be, then making mistakes, having things go wrong, losing a competition, they are supposed to happen?

Exactly!

Things go wrong (if that is what you want to say) so you can learn from the event. There is always a message and you gain when you study it.

However, using such words as mistakes, wrong or losing is just labeling. Those terms don't have to exist. Instead of mistake, try "progress by repetition." Instead of wrong, try "chance for a creative solution." Instead of losing, try "opportunity to study winning techniques."

Every event, every action, every thought is exactly what it must be in order for you to arrive at your intentions and desires. No matter how an event or action is labeled, no matter how you perceive it at the moment, it remains part of what is required in order for your desires and intentions to materialize.

No matter the event of the moment, you may choose to see it as correct or incorrect. The choice is yours, as are the consequences. However, if you are practicing the third secret, *practice non judgment*, you will not see it as either right or wrong, but as a learning experience.

Most the time, unfortunately, you label an event based on how it compares to past experiences.

But using past experiences to determine the correctness of a current event is almost always an ego choice. You quickly review past events to see if you lost control of the situation or were embarrassed by it. Your ego is making judgments. So whatever the present event, it will be tainted by how your ego perceived similar past occurrences.

Do not let your ego label events. Practice non judgment or you will never be able to accept the fact EVERYTHING IS EXACTLY AS IT SHOULD BE--the most difficult of the secrets to master.

Luckily, there is no requirement that you understand immediately the role of every event. You are only required to accept it as correct, for when you do, you will eventually discover the truth.

When you accept without judgment, knowing things are as they should be, you can learn, and then you can change things. This then is the importance of recognizing that everything is exactly as it should be, for in everything the lesson is there to help take you to your intended goals.

When you can accept everything as correct for

that moment, you can go beyond your ego, and release your creative potential.

You can accomplish anything, and therefore you can make a difference.

I've had plenty of difficulty trying to accept things as being exactly as they should be. I've fought frustrations, had terrible bursts of anger, lost my temper, jumped up and down, kicked my feet, behaved horribly and caused myself no end of troubles--with absolutely no success for the effort.

One of my desires was to have a small, but highly-proficient racing stable. I wanted a stable which produced enough income to keep the family financially comfortable, yet small enough I could personally train every horse. I wanted to have my hands on every horse every day.

It was a good program. So successful, in fact, new clients were knocking on the door nearly every week. In no time at all, I had quite a number of horses in race training and everything was booming.

My ego was exploding with joy.

When the new racing season started, I thought I had a pretty powerful stable and winning would be easy.

It didn't work that way. Everything that could go wrong started to go wrong.

Horses which should have won couldn't get close. Horses were suffering injuries which never should have occurred. Horses seemed to lose condition for no identifiable reason.

I worked harder and things got worse. So I worked harder still, and became more and more frustrated. My ego was suddenly directing the entire show. Everything I did to change the situation was ego-motivated. I wanted my clients to approve of my efforts and my training so I was constantly finding fault with others. The jockeys got the blame, the racing secretary wouldn't write the kind of races I needed, or my luck was just plain bad.

I simply did not want to accept the truth that everything was exactly as it should be. I wanted to fight it and make it different. I refused to look for the lesson being offered.

Several months passed with things continuing to decline. Finally, I stopped pandering to my ego and started to listen to my heart. I decided to accept the past problems as a message.

I looked at my stock, and wondered how and why I was training some of them. They had little talent, or problems which were obviously going to keep them from winning, or they simply needed to be at a race track where the competition was not so tough. They were getting beat by better horses and I was getting beat by smarter trainers. That was certainly exactly as it should have been.

The truth is often not nearly as difficult to see as it is hard to admit.

With a sizable stable, I simply did not have the time to handle every horse every day. I wasn't working my program, so things I did were not being done in the best interests of the horses. I was taking any horse in training because it boosted my ego, even though it worked against my intention. I wasn't giving, I was taking.

Things were a mess, and that is exactly as it should be if you are moving away from, rather than toward your intentions.

Pretty dramatic way to get my attention, but effective!

All the months of frustration, disappointment, blaming, worry and poor effort on behalf of the horses could have been avoided. All I needed to do was recognize the essence of the secret, accept things as being correct for the moment, learn from the moment and apply the lessons.

My desire was not to have a big stable, but a highly proficient one. My creative potential turned my big barn into a lesson which showed me how I had strayed from the path to my goals.

I culled the barn. Some of the horses were sold to go to smaller tracks, some became hunters, some trail horses and others just went home. I set a limit to the number of horses I would have, and I stuck to the limit.

The horses which remained in the barn ran in races they could win and with acceptable frequency, they did.

My original intention returned as reality. Once again I personally attended to every horse, every day.

Wishing things were different than they are accomplishes nothing.

Accept what is. Know the situation is what it should be and get on with what is required to create things as you want them to be. That is your creative potential at work, free from the destruction of ego.

105

Chapter six

The little naggy things that go wrong--the snap that breaks, hitting the log on a trail course, the wrong lead, a pulled shoe--those things are just telling you that you aren't in the moment.

You've lost focus.

Get your mind back on the job at hand, believe in what you are doing, concentrate, slow down, listen to your heart instead of the noise around you, and the little naggies will go away.

So how do things going wrong turn out to be exactly right for horses?

Horses do not reason, but learn from praise and punishment through repetition. They always seek comfort or avoid discomfort.

Although doing things correctly and receiving praise are important to the horse, they are not nearly as important as the mistakes he makes. It is the mistakes which lead to the real learning, because it is then that the communication is repeated and the message is reinforced.

There can be no learning without confrontation.

The first time you ask a horse to do anything, he may do it correctly. But since it was his first experience, he really doesn't know what it was he did. Did he turn his head, move a foot, swish his tail? He only knows he is getting praised, and he likes it.

However, when he makes a mistake, he meets with a confrontation. In this case it is verbal--the reprimand, "Ho!", and a repeat of the cue he didn't recognize the first time. He may not recognize the cue the second time, or the third or the fourth, but eventually he will perform the request, and he will be praised. He learns the communication because the confrontation gives him a way of understanding exactly what the desired response is. The praise is his reward for a good performance.

It is the perceived mistake which necessitates the repetition. It is the perceived mistake which leads to the learning. It is the perceived mistake (exactly as it should be) which advances the horse beyond the average and transforms him into a champion.

It is the mistake which makes the horse's training (the learning of a communication system) possible.

The mistake should not be answered by frustration, anger or loss of temper. Don't view the mistake as something bad or negative. Don't judge the mistake at all. Instead, accept it as a useful training aid or a signal for you to change your thinking or give new consideration to a situation.

When things go wrong, don't try harder. Don't try to force a solution or force the horse to learn. You can't whip, spur or jerk information into a horse. Just be smarter.

No matter what it is, it is exactly as it should be.

As hard as that is to understand, it is harder to accept and live.

As a trainer or rider of performance horses, you will discover each and every horse represents thousands of mistakes and problems which you must remedy. The answer to each mistake, each problem, lies within the experience itself.

Horses do communicate. They will tell you if they understand, if they are fearful, if they are comfortable, if they trust, and what they want and what they don't want.

They communicate through their behavior and actions.

The young green horse tells the trainer every day just how well he is progressing. Calm, mild acceptance of lessons previously learned means he is a student ready for more complicated and exacting performance. Happy, good-feeling horses are asking for more work, more physical activity and more competition.

A sour horse, a depressed horse, or a horse which refuses to perform up to level, should not be the object of a trainer's frustration and abuse. Instead, the trainer or rider must accept the horse as being exactly as he should be at that moment. The horse is communicating something to his partner which will never be understood unless the partner applies the secret.

So get into the moment.

Accept it; don't fight it.

Discover the truth.

The belief that everything is exactly as it should be is a requirement if your intentions and desires are to train or ride winning performance horses, or know the joy of a perfect partnership.

What you believe, you will achieve, and the choice is yours.

If you believe you will accomplish certain things, you will. If you believe you cannot achieve certain things, you certainly will not.

If you believe mistakes and problems and everyday difficulties prevent you from achieving your desires, that is exactly what will happen.

If you view mistakes and problems with your horse (or riding) as a chance to learn and correct, and then perform at a higher level, then that is what will happen.

Your power will bring about any desire you have, positive or negative.

If you see events and experiences as bad, they are bad.

If you see events and experiences as good, they are good.

The answer to how you perceive lies in your heart. It is possible to choose wrongly, but the result is never comfortable. Choose happiness for yourself and for your horse, and you will have chosen correctly. Then indeed everything will be exactly as it should be.

You, and you alone, are responsible for how you feel. You can change your feelings about any event or experience because you have the ability to change your thinking. You have the ability to feel good about every experience because you can choose to feel that way, and you can decide not to accept frustration, anger, disappointment, hurt or worry.

The attitude you take about an event will affect your actions and reactions, and your horse will learn from those events, whether positive or negative. The choice is yours.

Your horse eventually will reflect the result of your thoughts, your power, your creative potential. When you believe everything is exactly as it should be, then you will make enlightened choices as to how you will respond to every occurrence, and you will be in the moment, and you will act only in a way beneficial to your horse.

Any experience you fail to make positive for your horse steals from him. The horse is then the victim of negative experiences which you let happen. If for some reason the experience begins badly, it is your responsibility to transform it into a pleasurable one for both partners.

Only when you understand and accept everything as being as it should be can you apply the THIRD ELEMENT of training: COMPLIANCE THROUGH NONRESISTANCE.

Anything less than full acceptance of what is occurring becomes a resistance on the part of the trainer, the horse or both!

When you teach any horse to lead, you can first try to pull the horse forward, but he'll resist and pull back.

A different approach is to tug on the lead rope, immediately release the pressure, then tap the horse on the hindquarters with a whip. The horse will move forward. (All action initiates in the hindquarters.)

The first attempt to lead the horse resulted in a noncompliance by resistance. The second example shows compliance through nonresistance.

When a pressure is applied to the horse, one of two things will occur. The horse will push or pull back against the pressure, resisting, or he will move into a position of nonresistance.

To reach perfect horsemanship, the first reaction is never acceptable.

To reach perfect horsemanship, the second reaction, that of nonresistance, must always be the ultimate response of the horse.

Any cue given to a horse which requests a particular response always provides an opportunity for the horse to resist. The horse can ignore the cue (resistance from the mind). Or the horse can push back against pressure, or jump away from it. He can also buck, rear, or toss his head. He can grab the bit and run away, or refuse to budge (physical resistance).

Resistance is a refusal to comply willingly by either partner. In some cases, the resistance blocks the exercise from ever being completed. In other cases, the horse resists, but is overpowered and forced into finishing the task. Resistance on the part of the rider or handler is always expressed in a pulling or pushing action. The rider is pulling on the reins, or the handler is pulling on a lead. Resistance on the part of the horse is a pushing into pressure, or a bold attempt at total escape.

In the desired partnership between horse and rider, each has a specific duty. The rider always makes the requests for action, and the horse always responds.

Since the horse always responds, the horse can't initiate resistance to a request; he can only respond in kind to a resistance started and continued by the rider. The rider can pull back on the reins--always an incorrect action--and the horse can push back against the rider's hand. The rider can shift his weight, but not allow the horse to bring the pair back into balance, thus causing the horse to resist. Or the rider can give leg pressure cues, failing to discontinue the cue instantly once the horse responds. Failure to discontinue a cue immediately following a response is a faulty attempt by the rider to prevent the horse from making a mistake. Of course it leads to unwanted resistance.

So the responsibility for compliance through nonresistance lies with the rider.

The rider always initiates the possibility of resistance by giving a cue which requests a particular action on the part of the horse. To avoid resistance, the rider gives the cue, awaits responsive action on the part of the horse and discontinues the cue the instant the horse begins to respond.

However, the action by the horse may not be what the rider requested.

If the response is not what the rider wanted, the rider should not reprimand the horse, unless the horse is purposely defying the request. In the majority of cases during training, the horse has simply failed to understand the communication, and therefore should be given the request again. The cue should be discontinued again once the horse reacts. When the response is correct, the horse should be praised as the exercise continues. COMPLIANCE THROUGH NONRESISTANCE has been achieved.

Anytime there is a battle between horse and rider, whether it is mental or physical, there is resistance which needs to be removed.

At times, there is a need for a showdown. It occurs whenever there is a question as to who is going to make the requests, and who is going to do the performing.

When the horse questions who is making the decisions, it is time to set the record straight. The handler, trainer or rider must take disciplinary action. Such action can be anything from a good thump with the heel, to a series of bending exercises, such as rollbacks or shoulder-in. The horse's mind must abandon his first resistance and focus on the new exercises, eventually giving up all resistance.

The discipline should be well-planned, swift, appropriate and must end immediately upon compliance. Discipline which might cause serious or permanent injury to the horse certainly should never be used. The best forms of discipline are exercises which condition the horse's body as well as make him concentrate.

Such disciplines are necessary and they are a part of the training process, but should seldom be required. Always remember, you are not the master and the horse is not a slave. You are equal partners--each with a specific and equally important job to do. You decide what is to happen; the horse performs. Neither reaches perfection without the other.

Compliance through nonresistance should be the goal of every training session.

When the rider is "giving", then there will be no resistance on his or her part. When the horse understands and happily responds, there will be no resistance on his part. Then, and only then, can the partnership move toward being one mind, one spirit, one perfection.

Accepting the secret will change everything in your relationships with horses and the world of competition. You will catapult toward your goals. Success will rush toward you, and with it, different experiences to accept as being exactly correct for the existing moment.

As your riding and training become more perfect, and your successes as a trainer and rider multiply, you will come under increasing criticism from friends, clients and competitors.

This is normal. Those who do not know the secrets do not give, but attempt to take from others.

The higher you climb, the more frequently there will be those who constantly attempt to pull you down. They will say things, true or not, to discredit you. They will belittle accomplishments. They will go out of their way to tarnish your image. They are wasting their energy, and you should not waste yours in worry, concern or acknowledgment.

Nothing outside you can touch your spirit.

You lose your focus when you allow your ego (which is always seeking control over people or the approval of others) to give any attention to your detractors. It is not necessary that you have the approval of anyone, let alone those who would speak or work against you. You need only treat them with the same kind consideration you would offer anyone, and dismiss any of their criticism.

Then get on with your business.

Don't waste your time or energy talking or worrying about what others are saying or doing. Indifference on your part will keep you so busy you won't have time to be harmed.

How can such painful and cruel treatment from others be exactly correct for your moment?

By your choice. Choose to review and reaffirm the rightness of what you are doing. Double check your information, dig deeper for new knowledge, and ask your heart if you have made the correct choices.

If your heart tells you everything you are doing is in the best interests of the horses you are training and riding, then you never need give concern to acts or words directed against you or your success.

If you are in the moment, and you are complying with your nature by nonresistance, things are as they should be.

The desires you seek will be the reality of the moment.

Your intentions and desires will become your reality
when you are able to accept what is.

Chapter seven
You control your future

You have the power and some of the secrets, but you haven't yet attained perfect horsemanship.

Your horse is good, but his performances are not yet perfect and are sometimes erratic.

Why is the question.

Why is the answer.

Over the years, many have told me they wanted to be good riders or good trainers. Some even claimed they wanted to be champions.

Some asked for help, and I tried to be of assistance. Some asked questions, and I gave the best answers I could. Some became very good riders. A few are good trainers, and a couple have won championships.

Others want more--they want to know more than just "how". They demand to know "why?" And these special ones become the true masters, the ones who experience perfect horsemanship. They are the ones making riders, and performance horses and trainers better. They are the ones innovating and creating and writing the poetry.

Still, with all the joy and success which could be theirs, the vast majority just ride in circles.

Why is it some succeed and so many more fail?

It is because the failures only hope and wish for something better. They want things to be different, but they refuse to take action.

On the other hand, the successful, either knowingly or unknowingly, apply the SEVENTH SECRET: CREATE THE FUTURE THROUGH YOUR INTENTIONS AND DESIRES. The successful move forward; they make things different. They take action to make their future what they want it to be.

Intentions and desires are more than just pleasant ideas. They are more than just hopes and wishes. Intentions and desires are important choices made to be a part of your life.

Desires require clear and concise thinking. Intentions require determination.

First you must know what it is you want.

Do you know? Do you really know?

Do you actually have a true desire?

And if you do, do you intend for it to be a reality? Are you willing to take action to make it so?

Desires can usually be imagined almost like a movie. You can picture the color of the horse you are riding, the color and style of the jumps, the water obstacle, the course, and the faces in the crowd cheering for you. You can feel the horse under you, and at the same time you can see his legs in motion as he sets up for the jump, lifts and folds his knees as he goes up and over. You can see and feel yourself and your horse as you land, go on to the next jump and finish the course.

In your mind you can see yourself receiving your award, you can feel the exhilaration and you can understand the effort required for achievement.

It's important to see your desires as vividly as possible. Your mind doesn't know the difference between reality and imagination, so keep your mind visualizing your desires and your creative potential will make them factual.

During training sessions, riding lessons or coaching efforts, see every event unfolding perfectly. The more you see the perfection in your mind, the more you will see it in actuality.

Desires are generally short term. They may attract you for months or even a year or two. Your power will bring them about and once enjoyed, they will fade.

Intentions, on the other hand, may last a lifetime. Intentions require commitment. Intentions are long term, and if achieved, intentions spur you to learn more, and then to give more.

Intentions also require exact detail. You should be able to write down precisely what it is you intend to accomplish. You should know exactly how you will feel once you have achieved your goal. You should also be quite aware of the responsibilities which accompany success.

Bobbie Ellis intended to be a good rider.

She was so determined that at age 11 she

119

promised herself she would ride her horse and practice every day for one year. That's a tough promise for a little girl to keep, and it took a lot of sacrifice on her part and plenty of understanding from her parents.

For one year to the day, rain or shine, hot or cold, healthy or sick, alone or with help, she mounted up and rode her horse.

She kept her promise.

She both desired and intended. She created her future. She became an excellent rider who could sit a horse, any horse, as well as the very best I've ever seen.

Her intention became her reality.

If you want to be a champion, you must express the intention clearly to your spirit. As with desires, it is helpful to visualize the exact details. Play out your intentions again and again, making them so familiar you never miss a color or a sound as you watch your future.

Live your future every minute of every day.

Draw your future to you now.

Live your life this day knowing that all you want no longer awaits you, but is yours in this moment.

If you want your horse to perform perfectly, to win performance events, express your desire in unequivocal terms. Then you must ride the perfect ride; you must ride the competitions in your mind. Training sessions should become mental events.

When you start a training session, whether for yourself or your horse, begin it as if it were the biggest event of your life. Groom your horse and groom yourself. If you feel or look less than ready for perfection, then you won't reach perfection. If your horse believes he'll be asked for less than excellence, that's how he'll react. If he believes excellence is required, he'll deliver.

You transform your intentions and desires into reality by allowing your power of creative potential to change your future into your present. Believe and live as if it has already happened. You make your intentions and desires reality by living your future every minute, every hour, every day of your present.

When you live your intentions and desires, something wonderful happens mentally which changes your personality. Instead of being directed by your ego, trying to control events and force things to be as you want them, you will give control to your creative potential and accept things as they happen. You already know everything is exactly as it should be, and that everything is a part of the path to your destiny. Every activity, every deed has a message for you. Everything is an opportunity to learn the lessons necessary to make your intentions your reality.

When you let things happen instead of trying to force solutions or events, you begin to wonder why they occurred as they did, and what lesson they teach. So you ask, "why?"

And the answers provide insights which smooth the path.

The answers give you the understanding you

need to help your horse.

The understanding gives you confidence in yourself so you no longer need the acceptance or approval of someone else. You give up ego.

Once you begin to demand answers to the question, "why?", your world changes. Never again is "because," or "we always did it that way," or "take it or leave it, this is the way it is done," good enough. In your new world, you want answers which are supported by knowledge, either first-hand and/or scientific. You want answers which are supported by tangible evidence and from several sources.

You want answers which, when applied to your training or riding efforts, give actual and satisfactory results.

You want the answers which satisfy your heart.

Be willing then to dig out the information necessary to explain, "why."

Books, magazines and discussions with local and distant professionals will help answer your questions. You can learn much from many sources, and it is up to you to find the information. Don't be shy or timid. Go where you must to learn the truth.

And after you get your answers, be prepared to continue looking for evidence to support your beliefs while remaining open to new information and new ideas. Challenges to your answers are always welcome for they provide greater truths.

There are thousands of great teachers and horsemen ready, willing and able to help. The ones you want to learn from are those who are actually practicing what they preach. If they do exactly what they tell you to do, then it's a good bet they know "why" it works.

Don't accept any opinions about equipment, training or riding a horse unless the information is accompanied by an explanation of WHY it is the truth. But don't stop there. Gather supporting information of your own.

When you live each day as if your intentions have already become reality, you will listen to your heart and follow your heart. You will give instead of take, and your creative potential will make every event a perfect part of your journey.

Living your intentions and desires is the impulsion (forward force) which drives you toward your future.

IMPULSION, that forward driving force, is also the FOURTH ELEMENT of horse training, and a requirement for perfection.

You reach excellence in performance events by putting power into every movement of your horse. The power in the movement is delivered by impulsion.

Impulsion is not speed nor hurried movement. It is not tension. Impulsion results from an engagement of the horse's hindquarters. It can only be realized when the horse is driven forward to the bit, and then allowed to perform without interference.

The horse is driven forward by the use of strong leg and seat aids. The horse's action is initiated in the hindquarters by a lowering and forward movement of the hocks. The hindquarters then pick up more of the horse's weight, and propel the horse forward through an elastic swinging back and relaxed neck.

Impulsion is seen most easily in gaits which have a phase of suspension. The more impulsion the rider is able to produce, the longer in time, and/or distance, the duration of suspension. Trot and canter become lighter and more brilliant.

Impulsion is a requirement of every movement by every horse seeking perfection. Impulsion is evident as the horse drives his body forward with either grounded hind foot. Impulsion is as important in the walk of a reining horse as it is in the Piaffe or Passage.

It is difficult for many to understand that the slower the forward progress of the horse at work, the more the rider is required to apply consistent and constant leg pressure, driving the horse forward to elicit impulsion. It takes muscle strength for a horse to work with impulsion, and it takes a well conditioned rider to bring it about.

Rein cues, weight shifts and the changing of leg cues may communicate the next desired movement to the horse, but while in progress, they should not cause the impulsion cue to be abandoned. Impulsion, the forward force, must be continued throughout the movement. (Even when the horse is backing--which is controlled by a driving leg cue--impulsion is the power force.)

The key to impulsion is utilizing the minimum amount of power required for each movement while maintaining complete relaxation. Impulsion must be controlled so the horse remains on the bit without tension.

The half-halt is one of the most effective exercises for the development of a rider's ability to understand and produce impulsion in the horse. Driving the horse forward into a fixed bit position gives the rider a feel for the horse's power. Too much impulsion and the horse tenses, over flexes or pushes beyond the bit. Too little impulsion, and the horse does not shorten his body and slow his pace, but drops out of the gait, or stops.

No matter the riding discipline, impulsion is an element of a perfect performance.

Impulsion is elusive.

It can only be captured by a feeling.

Perfect performances are built on it.

With knowledge as a base and a feel for impulsion, you can propel yourself into your future. You will know in detail what you will accomplish, and you will have confidence in yourself and your ability to achieve.

Of course you cannot predict each event which will arise. You need only know and believe that each event is correct and is being directed by your creative potential. The important thing is to concentrate on how you react to each event. Your feelings are your responsibility. And you can change your feelings.

Suppose you don't win a competition. What emotions will you accept? Do you become depressed by defeat, or do you substitute the feeling there is something to be learned.

Depression is not a response from your heart. Being positive even in defeat is the right choice--a choice you have the free will to make. Being disheartened after a loss is a waste of your time and talent.

Suppose you win a competition?

Expressing elation at winning is a selfish response. Recognizing success and being satisfied with all its elements is a choice--a choice which will help you focus on making each element of the performance which contributed to your success even better in the future.

Being too joyful after a victory is ego-directed.

Winning and losing simply are. Accept them as lessons and apply what you learn.

Once you name your intentions and desires and begin your quest, you need never defend your choices.

Your confidence, your creative potential, your understanding that everything is exactly as it should be, plus the knowledge gained through study and struggle, make it unnecessary for you to explain to others your actions or the path you have chosen.

If you make your choices from your heart, your choices will be giving in nature. Your heart always knows right from wrong. Your choices will be correct.

If you ask "why" about every minute detail of a horse--from his diet, to his thinking, to his training, to his relaxation--and you ask "why" about every detail of the performance you wish to make, you will have greater contributions to give to any horse and to any performance. You will have greater insight into the world you have chosen. Greater insight means you can give more, and by giving more of yourself, you will speed the culmination of your desires and intentions.

Do not ask "why" because you believe knowledge will make you superior to others and thus a winner. Such thoughts are ego-driven and only diminish you. You may absorb more information than others, but the knowledge itself does not enhance you. The seeking is your reward.

Knowledge, of course, is of no value unless it is used, which means it is freely given and applied.

Telling someone you know all the answers means absolutely nothing, except you are a bore. Don't tell people what you know and don't use your knowledge to defend a position you have taken.

Show them your knowledge by giving!

Constantly seek new information, test it, and be sure it is the truth. Then give it away by demonstrating it in your care, training and riding of your horse.

Whatever truthful knowledge you have gained should be incorporated in any and all training and riding programs you undertake. And whatever the details of your equestrian programs, once established, they are uniquely yours. Stick with your program. Give it plenty of time to prove itself. Eventually the result will be the realization of your intentions.

Once you have made a decision to implement

a care, training or riding program of you own design, it is not necessary to convince others of its worth.

For example, you want to feed your horses the very best mixture of hays and grains to help them look and perform at their optimum Don't accept someone else's formula. Create your own feeding program based on the knowledge you have gained, tested and proven to be the right.

Horses doing different types and amounts of work need different amounts and types of feed. With study, you can arrive at the correct nutrients and digestible energy required by the individual horses in your care, based on the work expected of them.

Develop your feeding program, apply it and be ready to adjust it if necessary. Your horses, by their appearance, sleekness of coat, eagerness to work and overall health, will be the only needed validation of your program.

The answers you received to the question "why," gave you confidence of your knowledge, and therefore it is not necessary to defend your program or to convince others of the wisdom of your choices. Let those who did not ask or learn "why" succumb to the empty promises of the hundreds of advertising pitches for supplements, coat conditioners and energy enhancers.

Just as you learned about feeding programs by observing, asking questions and devising your own formula, you can learn about training your horse from the masters, if you believe their knowledge is right for you. Take cues, for instance. If you prefer a variation of an accepted cue, and you have tested and proven them to be satisfactory for you, use them. Pass on your knowledge and experience only if you are asked. It is never acceptable nor appreciated if, uninvited, you try to convince others of the truth of your discoveries.

If it is your intention to teach or coach others, then you will of course be imparting your knowledge, your beliefs and your opinions to those asking. Do so for the common good of all horses and horsemen, not to build or stroke your ego. Teaching is giving, not impressing. Teaching is the start of the awakening process for the curious. And if your teaching is truly giving, the student will soon be asking, "why?" When that happens, the teacher will recognize he or she has reached their destiny.

Searching for knowledge to help your horse, yourself or your students can take you down many paths. The choices you make during your quest are yours and yours alone. Along the way, you will seek the advice of peers, masters and charlatans. It is part of learning and is not to be avoided.

Everyone will have a message for you. Interpreting the message is your responsibility.

When you ask for information, give full consideration to that offered. But do not accept it as truthful or false until you have tested it with the question, "why?"

Trends and fads proliferate more rapidly today than they did yesterday. And with the explosive growth of the information industry, tomorrow will see even greater numbers of styles flashing before you.

Chapter seven

It is easy, even fun, to accept the latest equine fad. And for the most part, there is nothing wrong in doing so. It is part of the learning, examining, determining, maturing process. It is natural. But it can also be a starting place for the formation of a habit pattern which results in constant reaction rather than action.

Unfortunately, for the vast majority of riders and trainers, reacting and accepting without thought has become normal. They always follow the crowd rather than initiate.

Whatever is acceptable to the majority will be the way of the majority. But it won't be the way for those who will reach perfection in performance.

Performance horses, riders, trainers and coaches who reach perfection are the ones who initiate the fads and trends. They establish the styles for today and for tomorrow. Fashions, equipment and color and types of horses are the most easily-recognized fads in the horse world.

It seems everyone wears a western-styled hat that is popular at the moment no matter how it actually looks on the individual. Hats compliment or detract from certain shaped heads. Wear what looks good on you, not what someone else likes.

Don't be influenced by what others are doing.

Trying to look like a champion will not make you one. Champions do not let others dictate their choices. Champions innovate. Champions never choose to wear certain clothes, or use particular equipment, or ride popular styles simply because they believe they will gain the approval of their peers. Champions need only the approval of their own hearts.

Winners do not dress or ride in a style which makes them less attractive to a judge, even if the fashion or riding style is in vogue. Winners do not hide themselves in the crowd by wearing the camouflage of looking alike.

Winners play by the rules, and when certain standards are established, the winner measures up. If the standard or rule needs to be changed, the winner does so by acting for the common good.

Perfection is as unique as the individual who attains it.

Let's take a particular dressage show as an example. As you know, dressage competitions tend to be rather colorless.

Alice was riding a solid bay Thoroughbred mare with lots of talent, but none of the trendy warmblood look. Alice wore a small yellow ribbon in the braid of her hair which extended below the back of her cap. A legal adornment. Just before her first test, she was told she couldn't win with a yellow ribbon in her hair. She commented, "I was hoping this competition was based on the horse's performance."

It was. She won.

Just prior to her second test, she was informed by a seasoned competitor that while Alice's mare was nice, she needed a warmblood if she wanted to compete seriously.

Alice was not influenced by the opinions of others. She smiled, said, "Thanks," then proceeded to win the test, scoring above nine warmbloods.

I am not suggesting you flaunt change in the face of established standards. That was not what Alice was doing. She simply chose to let her performance speak louder than fads or fashions. Protests may call attention to areas needing change, but protests are not the forum chosen by those who seek perfection in horsemanship.

Attract attention as Alice did, by demonstrating knowledge and skill through the performance.

Change things by proving there is a better way.

There will always be those who freely give you their opinion or criticism, asked for or not.

Never be influenced by this. Requested advice is one thing. Unsolicited trash talk is another.

The opinions of others are usually offered in the disguise of support. On occasion, such pronouncement may be intended to be helpful. But if you feel you need that opinion or want it, you are allowing yourself to be ego-directed. You do not need opinions which support or detract from your position.

Letting opinions influence your choices is to ignore the secret of choosing from the heart.

Do not be influenced by the criticism of others. Such criticism is never of value, even when it is called constructive. It will do you no service, nor will it help your horse, nor your performance. Criticism, even if self-directed, is negative and detracts from that which is there to be learned.

Remember, every event is exactly as it should be. You know what the event was. There is no need to listen to the criticism of another, since the important message has already been delivered by your creative potential, and it is solely for you to grasp its meaning.

You know if you performed less than perfectly. You don't need to be told. You know if your horse did not do his best, and you will explain it to your horse, calmly and positively, in the next training session.

Don't ask for criticism.

If criticism is forced upon you, listen without comment. Never be influenced by it. You will be influenced by your own truth soon enough.

Only you know of your true destiny.

Only you know of the impulsion which drives you ever forward.

And you are the only one who can interpret the feeling within your heart.

Your future is what you decide to make it.

Living it now is the way you attain it.

Even when things seem wrong they are correct.
Seek acceptance and nonresistant compliance.

Chapter eight
Surrender to uncertainty

Your future is created through your intentions and desires.

All things are possible when you surrender to your creative potential.

Surrendering means you stop trying to control every situation and begin to accept what is.

Surrendering is victory.

Only when you accept what is, can you create what will be.

There must be a hundred different kinds of performance horses. Each discipline has its own style, its own set of standards, its own heroes and champions.

Trainers of the different types of performance horses tend to use somewhat the same techniques, similar equipment and approximately the same exercise routines. Riders of jumpers usually follow the same established advice in their attempts to succeed. Reining horse riders use pretty much the same teaching aids to get a good spin. Race horse trainers haven't changed their methods much in the past 250 years.

Fundamentally, every horse is the same. So when you get right down to it, there are a limited number of practical ways to work with the horse. What you see is what you get. The basic anatomy of all horses is identical, and while all horses are individuals, they all move, react and learn in about the same manner.

The basics are always the same, and the dressage (basic dressing) masters have defined and explained all the movements of the horse. They have recorded all the necessary cues and aids. So if you study dressage, you will have the foundation knowledge to train any horse.

It really is that simple.

All horses trot, but the western pleasure horse both trots and jogs. The jog is a modification of the trot, the same as the western pleasure lope is a modification of the canter. The cues for either come from dressage. The western pleasure horse differs from the hunter, roper, reiner or barrel racer in style of movement. The same can be said of the flat racer, the three-day eventer and the coach horse--each is an individual, yet each is similar. While each has stylized movements, the cues and training are fundamental.

So what makes a champion in any specific event?

Uniqueness!

The champion horse, the best, the superior

Accept uncertainty

performer, does what all the other horses do, but this horse does it better, and he does it with a special grace and in a unique way. The same is true of outstanding riders or teachers.

Uniqueness is defined as "singularity, like no other." Uniqueness exists outside all groupings. It exists alone. It is independent. Uniqueness is not physical. It is mental. It comes from a thought.

You have a human form, but what makes you uniquely you is a thought.

A horse has an equine form, but what makes the individual horse a unique personality is the 'heart' within.

The champion horse and rider perform within the uniformity of the competition, but are never the same as the other performers. Their perfect rides and horsemanship are seen in the physical action, but arise from the uniqueness created by the combination of the mental powers of horse and rider.

Certain conformation may contribute to the making of a fast horse or a jumper or a reining horse. Conformation affects the soundness of all horses, and yet no conformation (form) assures a champion. A champion horse must have the 'heart' to win. 'Heart' is intangible. It is difficult to define. It cannot be captured or created. It is the same as the creative potential within you.

And so to reach perfection in performance, you must be aware of and focus on both your form and the horse's form while your creative potential translates thoughts into action.

The EIGHTH SECRET will help you do that. It

137

Chapter eight

is: ACCEPT UNCERTAINTY AND GIVE UP YOUR SEARCH FOR SECURITY.

This secret is most likely the exact opposite of what you've previously been told. The prevailing advice is to change uncertainty into certainty (security).

But that's impossible.

Your next moment is uncertain. It can't be predicted or controlled. Consequently, there is no security. Security is a myth. The only security, if there is to be such a thing, is in giving up security as a concept and accepting uncertainty.

You must be willing to give up the known, go beyond the fear, and accept the unknown.

You know your horse will act differently every day, every week, every year. You too will be different by the hour. New information, new experiences, increased practice, a changing of your ideas, all contribute to your own metamorphosis. You cannot stop it.

The only constant is change.

It is the way of our universe and all things therein and beyond. When you accept uncertainty, you stop attempting to be your ego's image and you become your unique self. Instead of seeking the approval of others, you use your special talents to create and initiate. No longer do you need the comfort of being the same as others.

There are those who suggest attention to self, having desires for the future and believing in my earlier assurance that you are as important, as intelligent and as uniquely gifted as anyone else, are forms of selfishness.

The great thinkers of our history agree that knowing one's self is the first step to being of benefit to others and all things. However, knowing self should not mean indulging in egotism, but should be an examination and understanding of one's creative potential.

Knowing self is acknowledgment of your strengths and weaknesses, identification of your unique talents and acceptance of responsibility for your choices and actions.

Once you know your self, you embrace your creative potential. You don't make judgments. You give instead of take and you become truly unselfish, for you will then always be completely independent and never a burden to someone else.

Know yourself and believe in your creative potential and you can go beyond fear.

Accept uncertainty and you can discover your unique self and when you do, you move toward perfection in horsemanship and all you do.

While you are learning to accept the uncertainty in all endeavors, there is one thing of which you can be certain. Once you have established your goals, your creative potential will guarantee their accomplishment. If you truly intend for them to come about, they shall be completed. Only the changing of intentions can change the path of your quest. You alone have that option.

Let's say you have started the journey to perfection in horsemanship. You have set goals as a rider, a teacher or as a trainer. You are living each moment of your future now, knowing the power of your creative potential. At this moment, the events which will take you to your final destination are being formulated. Each happening will have special meaning, a message, a special method of transport. Each happening will be exactly as it should be.

It is not necessary you recognize each incident and understand it instantly. In time you will look back and see it for what it was, what each event always is--an opportunity for learning.

Accepting what is means you will not try to hang on to what you wanted an event to be. You will not be frustrated and angry because the event was less than you had hoped. And you will not be overly joyful when an event is more than expected.

The easiest way to accept what is, is to give up your attachment to specific expectations.

When you go out in the morning to work your horse, even if you do not have a detailed plan, you have a general idea of what you want to accomplish or what new exercise you want to teach. You have established an expectation for yourself and for your horse. That is fine. The expectation is a goal; it is a measuring mark. The expectation, however, is not to be demanded. Seldom do expectations materialize exactly as you envision them.

Horses, and even riders, do not conform like a piece of clay into preconceived notions of how things will be. The goal may be reached, but the path is never without twists and turns.

It is helpful to see perfection in your mind before you start. Perfection is the goal. Visualize the horse working perfectly, and the rider giving all the correct cues with subtlety. Such mental assistance is an excellent aide during any training session.

However, a training session is for training, development and refinement, and is not meant to be perfect. The mistakes, the tiny steps of progress, the successes are part of the journey, and are to be accepted as they are--simply a part of the process.

If you can give up your attachment to specific expectations, you will also be giving up the anger and frustration associated with failure. By accepting events as they occur instead of demanding an exact result, you eliminate any failure to achieve and replace it with a step toward the future.

You can accept all events with confidence, knowing that they are not stumbling blocks, but stepping stones to accomplishment. You will have surrendered to your creative potential, and therefore will be receptive to the positive messages of the moments. You will accept the imperfections, and in doing so, you can "give" to the horse and to yourself, the inspiration needed to move forward.

Horses learn by repetition based on both reward and confrontation. Unfulfilled expectations during training sessions provide the opportunity to repeat the cues, the aids and the exercise. The horse gains, the rider gains, the trainer gains and the teacher gains. The mistakes and imperfections are part of a perfect plan.

However, if you remain attached to specific expectations, there can only be frustration and anger when goals are not realized.

Chapter eight

Frustration and anger are products of the ego, and when the ego takes control, physical abuse too often follows as attempts at forced control tear the partnership apart.

When you cannot let go of your expectations, damage to horse, rider, trainer and teacher is the final result. Such damage is frequently both mental and physical. Fortunately, in most cases it is repairable by repeated training sessions of care and giving which restore the horse's confidence and trust. The only thing which can be said positively for frustration and anger is that they deliver exactly the right message for the moment-- "You must give up your attachment to specific expectations."

And until you do, the message will be repeated again and again.

I have suffered the same frustrations over and over again by refusing to accept the message. Looking back, it seems many times I did my best to prolong my misery.

Actually, I was both refusing to accept the message and refusing to surrender to the moment. My refusals sustained my pain and ignorance and caused the horses unnecessary hurt.

At an early age, I had been conditioned to believe my ego could make things happen and I was determined to prove I could. I only proved I could not.

It is never the baser ego, but always the higher power of creative potential which brings about your desires and intentions.

Speaking of expectations, there will be times

you will find yourself in competitions you are certain you will win. Sometimes you will win (favorites win 33 per cent of the time) and sometimes you won't.

But if you have given up your attachment to specific expectations, you won't be disappointed at the loss. Likewise, you will not be overly jubilant with a victory. It is best for you, your horse or your students if you remain serene either way.

It is not wrong to establish goals and expect to achieve them. Expection of achievement is the driving force, the impulsion which moves you closer to accomplishment. There are the goals of attending futurities, annual shows, schooling events and championships. These are goals of preparation. Everyone recognizes that in order to reach perfection in horsemanship both horse and rider must be prepared, experienced and ready.

Goal setting is a way to measure progress and achievement, to know when you are ready. Only in this way is the specific expectation of reaching the goal acceptable.

Goals are the building blocks of a horse's training program.

Leg yielding, once accomplished, leads to renvers and travers, while other lateral work leads to side-passing and spins. Each movement might be the goal of a week or month's training. When the goal has been reached, the horse is ready to move on to more complicated exercises.

Most horses will eventually learn the basics, but the basics will not be enough to carry you to the higher levels of horsemanship. You must recognize and accept the fact that some horses learn the basics but cannot perform at advanced levels. If you want to reach a higher level of horsemanship, such horses must be released.

Trainers and riders who fail to recognize the horse's limitations cannot advance because they refuse to release the limited horse and begin again with a more capable candidate. Attachment keeps them from perfection.

Releasing attachment to specific expectations removes a barrier to freedom--freedom to change, freedom to learn and freedom to travel the path being constructed by your creative potential.

When you give up specific attachments, you develop a "suppleness", an ability to adjust as you accept what is.

Likewise, "SUPPLENESS" IS THE FIFTH ELEMENT of a horse's training.

Suppleness is not looseness and it is not flexibility. It indicates an advanced stage of training for the unrestricted horse.

A horse is said to be unrestricted if he accepts his rider without tightening his back muscles and then willingly begins a well-timed trot without rein contact. He must also continue the trot with relaxed body and back muscles, maintain a pleasant expression, ears half erect in attention to the path and the rider and carry his tail with a natural swinging rhythm.

Suppleness develops from this state. It is initiated by the requested and more forceful driving action of the hindquarters as the horse stretches forward to reach the bit. The mouth, poll and neck should yield.

The supple horse has the ability to shift his balance point forward and back, as well as from side to side without stiffness or resistance. He is pliable. This is seen in his adjustments of carriage (longitudinal) and (lateral) bend. The supple horse is moldable and can be rounded and shaped.

Suppleness is most easily seen in transitions from gait to gait. As the horse's body shortens or lengthens in response to the changing engagement of the hindquarters, the supple horse responds smoothly and seemingly without effort.

Stiffness is the opposite of suppleness and is easily witnessed or felt when the horse is unable to drive his hindquarters under himself in downward transitions. The stiff horse will leave his hind legs rigidly behind and throw his balance into the rider's hands as he looks for support.

Suppleness is dependent upon and stimulated by impulsion. Suppleness is complete when the energy of the horse flows from the hindquarters through the cues given by the rider and into the requested movement. The truly supple horse will be filled with power, but will be completely relaxed, and will chew the bit correctly--soft and easy, with no sound, but with an increase of saliva in the mouth.

A horse which grinds his teeth, or tries to hold the bit with his teeth, is showing the signs of psychological or physical discomfort, and is not supple.

The half-halt is the best exercise to test for

suppleness. If the horse gives an instant response to the half-halt cue, then the horse is supple and ready for a transition of gait. If the instant response is not forthcoming, the horse is not supple, and the transition should not be executed. Repeat half-halt cues until instant response is elicited, then make the transition.

Shoulder-in is the most effective exercise for the improvement of suppleness. However, lateral work of any kind is also beneficial.

A supple horse is one ready to respond to any situation with full energy of purpose, yet with complete relaxation.

A supple horse is not searching for security, for he is pliable in the moment. So too are riders and trainers of horses which reach perfection.

If those seeking perfection wanted security, they would not attempt to improve themselves or their horses. They would not expose themselves to the possibilities of failure.

Seeking security is seeking the mediocre. It is seeking the safety of being accepted and approved by everyone. It is totally ego-driven. If you want to reach perfection with performance horses, give up the idea of the supposed comfort of security.

Accept the risks; take your chances.

Have you ever noticed how often people talk about, either to praise or criticize, the top riders and the top horses at a competition? While you hear about the winners and the top competitors, you never hear about or even participate in discussion about the riders and the horses which consistently finish in the bottom third of the class.

Have you ever stopped to consider that those riders and horses which are near perfection have no security? Everyone wants to end their reign. They are always the target.

Those in the bottom third of the class have security of a kind. They are not a threat to their fellow horsemen so they are perfectly acceptable and therefore meet with approval--for the present.

The insecurity of being on or near the top always exists, and even the shallow security of underachieving is short-lived. You either get better or eventually recognize you don't really intend to improve. If you get better, you become a threat to weaker individuals and you immediately lose your security. If you find something else to do, you enter a learning period and again have no security.

Security is impossible, but is a idea which nearly everyone has been conditioned to believe is the prerequisite to peace and prosperity.

What part of your life can you identify as absolutely, positively secure, and in no danger of changing unless you so will it?

Once examined, security vanishes.

Now try to define security as it applies to your intentions and desires within the world of horses.

Has the day ever existed in which you enjoyed absolute security?

Of course not!

You have been secure only in a moment, because a moment is all you have, and all you ever will have. The past is gone and cannot be regained.

147

Chapter eight

It can be experienced again and again as a thought, but can never actually exist again as reality.

The future is not yet yours.

It may never be.

Accept the idea you have nothing more to gain nor to lose than the moment you are in now, so make the most of the moment.

The experience of perfect horsemanship is just beyond your fear of failing.

Experiencing no fear, taking chances, working without a net, is the way of winners, those who will innovate. They are the masters who establish the styles and the standards. They fear nothing from their peers, for they seek neither acceptance nor approval. They are secure in their moment.

They accept the necessity of going beyond the known, and they are willing to make a total commitment. If they fail, they were not seeking the security of mediocrity, but the perfection of art.

I do not mean to say those who seek perfection do ego-driven crazy, foolish or dangerous things. To do so would be uncharacteristic of one who knows the secrets. The perfect horseman gives to his partner, never endangering him.

But equestrian sport is action and power, and there will be injuries. Accept that fact, or accept never being an innovator, a master or a seeker of perfection.

Those who attain perfection always seek perfection. Anything less is not an option. There is no holding back, no hoping or wishing or praying. Instead, there is action. Perfection seekers go to the edge. They go beyond the known, They attack; they never saddle up willing to accept less than perfection.

Peter accepts the danger and the uncertainty of horsemanship. He long ago gave up the search for security and his attachment to specific expectations.

As an Australian farm boy, he had the security of land and work. But Peter wanted to be a horse trainer. He arrived in the United States with very little money (practically none), no place to live, a short visa and a lot of determination. I don't need to tell you it was tough for him. There were family problems, government problems, no credit, no work history. But he had a saddle and a bridle.

He had a lot of downs, and he got bounced around pretty hard by life for the next couple of years, but he made it.

He's pretty good with a jumper and he has galloped race horses with me. He has started hundreds of young horses and he is known to be a good hand with rough stock.

Peter now trains western horses, makes a living, has a family, and still accepts things as they come. I don't know for sure if he has achieved all his intentions and desires. I only know I have a lot of respect for the man and his accomplishments.

Peter lost his right arm in a farm machinery accident when he was a small boy.

Next time your determination wanes, or you feel a twinge of insecurity, try putting a halter on your horse using only your left hand.

All things are possible.

Go beyond the fear.

You have within all you need.

Even at the moment of greatest effort and triumph,
the minds and bodies are in perfect balance.

Chapter nine

Require nothing. Give everything

Eliminate ego and you will be independent.

If you are independent, you will not search for security.

Do not seek security and you require nothing from others.

If you require nothing from others, you are without ego, and therefore free to give.

Success is easy!

Failure is hard.

Everyone has a special talent.

Whatever your special talent, you are better at that particular something than anyone else in the world. It may be hard to accept, and it may seem a little less than humble, but it is a fact.

Your special talent is a gift. It is part of your creative potential.

What is your specific flair?

I don't know, and maybe you don't either--yet.

But success is easy, and failure is hard, and therein lie the first clues to your distinctive ability.

Chapter nine

Whatever it is, you will label it easy, fun, joyful and fascinating. So begin by looking at all the things you like. If you love horses, begin by looking at the things you like doing best with horses.

Select the things which are easiest for you, and reject those chores which are difficult. (Things which are difficult often end in failure because they are drudgery, unpleasant and stiffling. To face such things daily is hard, and that is why failure is hard.) When you reject the difficult and unpleasant things and turn to the things which make you happy, you will begin to get a clearer idea of your special talent.

Here's another clue to finding your gift. Once you recognize it, you will never think of it as work. It may later turn out to be the thing you dedicate yourself to for life. You may call it your vocation or your choice. But even if it eventually takes on the name "employment," you will never see it as work. For convenience, you may call it work or you may call it your job, but you will always see it as something you want to do, something you must do, something you love to do.

Those who find their special talent, then make that talent the central theme of their daily efforts, are the most successful people in the world. They may not be the most wealthy in terms of dollars, but they will be rich in all that matters. They will have tasted perfection. And they can never quite get enough of it. They don't need vacations. They don't need awards. They don't need encouragement; they just want to keep doing.

It is very important you discover your special

talent, for finding it is part of the final secret of perfect horsemanship. The last SECRET is: "FIND YOUR TALENT AND USE IT TO BENEFIT OTHERS."

If you are in the equestrian field, others will be people and horses. In both cases, when you use your special talent to benefit others, you become perfect. So do the horses and so does the world.

While you are in the process of deciding what you like to do best, you may think you are being diverted from your original goal of reaching perfect horsemanship. You may not recognize how what you are beginning to perceive as your gift can possibly lead to your intentions and desires.

When you discover your unique skills you may be shocked to discover also that very often they do not lead to the goal you think you should seek to attain. Very often the goals named are named for the wrong reasons, and are not your true desire. Sometimes the things we really want are suppressed due to pressures from outside forces.

Many times peers, parents or friends cannot understand and accept the dreams of others. It is because they are making judgments, have different intentions and desires and are ruled by their ego, seeking to control and win approval.

If those close to your do not approve of your dreams, do not hide your feelings. Do not conceal your true desires.

Be brave and follow your heart. To abandon your desires simply to avoid conflict or ridicule is a mistake. To turn away from your true talent to please someone else results in no one being pleased.

Chapter nine

You are not required to do the bidding of others, so do not fight your inclinations. Accept your apparent natural ability to excel as a sure sign you should pursue that talent with all your heart. Your heart will soon tell you if you are doing the correct thing, for your heart's answers are never wrong.

I had a student who wanted to ride competitively and win. Unfortunately, she lacked talent as a rider and she had no ability to train a horse.

Still, she loved the horses. She loved the competition and she loved being with all the people at shows. She did not want to give up her dreams, but it was pretty obvious all that love would never make her a winner as a rider.

In desperation, she decided it wasn't that her horse was not good enough, or that she wasn't an accomplished rider.

She decided she just didn't have the look it took to win. So she made up her mind to create another kind of look. By creating a new style of show clothing, she believed she could become a winner.

Immersed in her new project, she found her special talent.

She soon came to the realization that she might not have the ability to show horses, but she had a knack with the sewing machine, and she could make others look good in the ring. She could create eye-catching fashions, and she did.

Within a few months, she was designing and

making clothes for some of the top competitors on the west coast.

She was a winner in the performance horse world.

She had satisfied her heart's desire.

But did she realize her original intention of riding and winning?

She had given up competitive riding and was happy in the business she had created. She had never been happy in the show ring. Competing on performance horses was hard for her, and in all practical terms, she was a failure at it. Designing and making clothes was easy for her, and she was a great success at it. She was happy.

You decide if she reached perfection in the show ring.

Generally people tend to think of tasks that are hard for them to do as "work."

Because most people are told they must work, (meaning they must do things they don't like) most people think it is their obligation to bring in a paycheck, to do whatever is available, no matter how much they dislike it. It is their job, right or wrong.

It is unfortunate, but true, that most people in the wrong jobs will never escape. They simply can't grasp the idea they can make a living doing something they like.

You should make it your choice that your work, your business, is a natural expression of your talents and personality.

There is no doubt, no question, no debate, that you will be more successful doing something

155

you like rather than doing something you don't like.

You will always do a better job at tasks which are easy for you than you will at a task which is difficult.

If it is necessary for you to make a living, you can, you will, by using your distinctive ability. There is no acceptable excuse for not using your talent. Any excuse offered which your heart rejects is positive confirmation you have found your niche.

You may have the idea you want to be a horse trainer and you may like training horses.

But perhaps you spend more time talking about training horses than you do actually training them. You like intellectualizing. You like to understand the logic behind the movements, cues, the learning process and the ultimate performance. And you like explaining all this to others.

Your special talent might lie in teaching. But teaching what? A specific type of horse? A particular exercise? Children, adults or the specially gifted? Who knows?

You know. The answer is in your heart.

Your initial intention may have been to be a trainer of performance horses. You might find yourself on a different path as you discover teaching is easy, but training is not. However, that may not be the end. Remember, nothing is by chance and everything is exactly as it should be. It just may be you need to be a teacher for awhile in order to learn the lessons necessary for you to become a top trainer of performance horses.

As you gain knowledge and insight, you may

not want what you initially thought you wanted. Then again, you might.

Success is easy, so take the easy way.

Failure is hard, as you will discover and rediscover every minute you do something you don't like doing. If it is difficult for you to perform, stop the activity and find something within your area of interest which is easy, exciting and fun.

Don't for a second believe you cannot exchange the drudgery of work for the joy of doing what you love. You can escape. You will escape the very second you announce your intentions, and dedicate yourself to living your future in this moment without a thought for security.

Don't be misled. You still have to take action and put forth tremendous effort. But it will be a different kind of effort--the kind you can't wait to get started and hate to stop. You will put in the hours and the effort because it is what you want to do.

However, it will not all be horse treats. There will be the anticipated good times and unexpected bad times. As we know, everything is exactly as it should be, so good times, mixed with bad times, are complimentary and produce a harmonious unity. If there are contending forces, there are also cooperating powers.

It is imperative we have opposing events. Recognizing the opposites in events, feelings and actions is a step in the process of transformation and change. Opposites are required, for in opposites are the answers you seek. Opposites help you find your way to perfection in horsemanship.

157

For example, if you want a horse to be able to move forward slowly, help him to develop the required strength by having him move backward rapidly. If you want a horse to be able to change leads smoothly and quickly as he changes direction, teach him to hold a lead and counter-canter effortlessly.

Look for answers in opposites, for in opposites there is balance, therefore harmony.

And it is within the harmony and balance between partners that we find the SIXTH, and final, ELEMENT OF HORSE TRAINING--COLLECTION.

There are plenty of explanations of collection. The most frequently repeated definition relates almost exclusively to dressage, or "l'Equitation d'Ecole--high school riding." Almost all dressage explanations begin with the idea the horse's forehand must always be elevated. This is because dressage horses, at the higher levels, carry themselves within a shortened frame, created by an elevated forehand and lowered hindquarters. Western horses, however, do not elevate the forehand, but instead lower it in many instances.

Cutting horses are an example of collection in opposition to the traditional view of dressage.

I believe collection might best be characterized as being a state in which the horse relieves the forehand by increasing the load on the engaged hindquarters to bring about a perfect balance for a specified purpose.

In order to attain this state of collection, the horse will be on the bit (with or without rein contact), his hindquarters moved forward, back muscles elastic and spine rounded upward. Such balance must be achieved with or without a rider to be considered true collection.

While standing, a horse's natural balance point is just behind and slightly above the elbow. If a rod were pushed through the horse's body at this point, the horse would balance. There is less horse in front of the rod, and more horse behind the rod because the horse naturally carries nearly 60 per cent of his weight on the forehand. This natrual balance point is just in front of the rider's body.

In collecting the horse, the rider must ask the horse to engage the hindquarters, picking up some of the rider's weight, and some of the forehand weight, so the new balance point is moved under the rider.

It takes a strong, athletic horse, well-schooled in the previous five elements of training, to collect to this degree. But once having attained this degree of collection, the horse is capable of moving forward, backward or to either side in perfect balance for a specified purpose. A horse collected to this degree can move as a jumper, a park horse, a western pleasure horse, a rope horse, a dressage horse, a race horse or a cutting horse.

Because he is balanced, he raises or lowers his head and neck in order to perform a specified action.

Whether or not there are higher degrees of collection is debatable. Not all horses are capable of even partial collection. Conformation plays a role in collection. Athletic ability plays a role, and so does mental attitude.

But in all cases of attempted collection, the goal remains the same--balance, so whatever the requested action, the performance response will be easier. (Success is easy.)

Collection for one particular purpose can be different from collection for another reason. But no matter the exercise, collection is essential to perfect horsemanship.

When horse and rider are in balance, there is a unity which becomes a power in itself. On the other hand, lack of balance and discord result in ineffectiveness.

Remember that training and thought will always be in a state of flux. Things will always be changing or developing, but won't necessarily be moving you forward. You cannot look upon your training as progress, or the horse's mistakes as regression. There will always be both, from both partners, and that becomes part of the process of achieving perfection.

Kept in balance, positive and negative forces correct the inadequacies and excesses of the other, and a true partnership results in thought and performance.

The process is actually all there is.

A show or a competition is only a brief look at the process in continuation. And during this part of the process, specific labels should be meaningless to the partnership. A win is not a win, and a loss is not a loss. Both are experiences, training sessions for the partnership which seeks perfect horsemanship without the need for a label.

The partnership will reach the state of collection--pure balance--when competition means not trying to be better than other participants, but instead is singularly the process of you and your horse moving toward perfection. The competition is then only to be better than you've been.

You will be in balance when you eliminate all consciousness of the event, and simply remain in the process of being a partner to your partner.

You, your horse and the partnership provide the balance necessary for a pure state of harmony.

You will be in balance when you believe and accept your creative potential and are able to eliminate your ego so your heart makes the choices. You will be in balance when you can practice non-judgment, making choices of giving as a response to everyone and everything. You will be in balance when you accept the fact everything is exactly as it should be, and you can therefore accept uncertainty. You will be in balance when you can give up the search for security to pursue the search for your special talent. You will be in balance when you choose to give your talent, time and efforts to benefit others.

Make the choice to be in balance.

Knowing what is required of you to be in balance reveals the final ingredient for a perfectly balanced partnership. To reach perfection in horsemanship, the horse must be perfectly suited to the performance. He must be talented at the event

161

chosen and he must want to give to his partner.

Success for a horse is also easy. Failure for a horse is also hard.

It is in finding the horse's talent that true love for a horse and horses is discovered. If you say you love horses, and then attempt to make a horse perform at an event or level for which he is not suited you are not showing love. You are demonstrating selfishness and your action is ego-directed, merely taking. Sell the horse, give the horse away or simply care for him for the rest of his life, but stop trying to make a jumper out of a western trail horse. It can be done, but it will be hard, and the horse will be a performance failure. There will be no harmony or balance.

The most successful race horse of modern time, Cigar, winner of more than $9 million, has a pedigree which indicated he would love racing on the grass. He did not. In fact, as a grass horse, he was rather average.

So his owner and his trainer tried him at something different. When switched to a dirt track, his special talent was revealed, and he reeled off no less than 16 consecutive victories, beating the very best of his day.

Given the right circumstances, success is easy for horses. When performing that for which they are naturally talented, they do it easily, willingly and well.

Horses are more limited than you in areas of talent. A horse's special ability will be in a type of movment, for that is the gift all horses were given by nature. Find the horse with the mental attitude and the correct movement for the event you want, and then establish a partnership. Do not establish a partnership and then try to make the horse into something he is not.

Those who truly love horses can part with a horse when they know the horse will get a chance elsewhere to find his talent. It is not kind nor loving to continue with a horse which is not happy doing the work demanded of him.

A competition horse, performing at his best, is in harmony and balance. He will, most likely, be victorious when four requirements are met.

First, the horse cannot be in any kind of pain.

If asked, a horse will perform, even with pain. But he cannot perform at his best. Unlike a human, he does not envision a reward for doing something he feels is foolish.

Correct the problem causing the pain, or do not ask the horse to perform. If the problem cannot be corrected, the only choice is to change horses.

The wrong choice of masking pain so performance may continue is often done, even advised and condoned by those who should know better. It is always the wrong choice, ego-driven and selfish. The choice to ignore what is best for the horse makes perfection impossible.

Second, the horse must be fit to do the job.

Over-training is common and a major problem with performance horses. The horse's efforts become listless when he is worked too hard and too often. Over-training always leads to a breakdown of the horse's skeletal or muscular systems.

A fit horse does his job, then has quick heart and respiratory recovery rates. The task a fit horse performs does not stress him excessively.

Third, the horse must have adequate rest.

Too many performance horses are worked again and again before an event so they won't have an edge and make silly spooky mistakes. Horses which need to have the edge taken off have not been trained adequately, or the trainer/rider is seeking security rather than perfection. A horse which has not had adequate rest cannot give a brilliant, winning performance. He simply won't feel good enough to reach perfection.

Finally, the horse must be asked to perform at a level at which he can succeed. Overmatching a horse is the surest way to fail in the attempt for perfection.

Success is easy. If the competing horses are not as good as the horse you are riding or racing, your horse will usually win. Failure is hard. Make it difficult for the horse to win and soon the horse, the rider and the trainer fall short.

The partnership will be balanced only when both partners willingly give their talents. If you have found your special talent, and you have found the horse with the particular gift for the event you have chosen, and each is giving for the benefit of the other, perfect horsemanship is inevitable.

But if in finding your talent, you realize your intentions to reach perfection in horsemanship were not lasting, but were in fact just passing fancies, no matter. You can still find perfection in other areas.

You are special, unique, as important as anyone else, whether you win worldwide acclaim, or you go quietly about giving to others.

You know that now.

Giving of your talent to benefit others is in itself the greatest perfection possible. Giving your talent to benefit others makes you perfect.

The nine secrets of perfect horsemanship are now yours. Apply the secrets and all the potential you possess will inevitably turn dreams to reality.

Wherever you are now is exactly where you have placed yourself. You are exactly where you should be at this moment.

The next moment is yours.

The choices are yours. The truth is in your heart.

If your future perfection is with horses, that's wonderful. If it is not, it's still wonderful.

Allow the secrets to take you anywhere you desire to go, to be everything you intend to be.

The Nine Secrets

1. Your creative potential exists.
2. Let your heart decide.
3. Practice non-judgment.
4. Give.
5. Choose how you respond.
6. Everything is exactly as it should be.
7. Your intentions become your future.
8. Accept uncertainty. Give up security.
9. Find your talent. Act to benefit others.

The Six Elements

1. All action initiates in the hindquarters.
2. Communication.
3. Compliance through non-resistance.
4. Impulsion is power in movement.
5. Suppleness produces grace in action.
6. Collection controls balance.

Clip this page and post it on bathroom mirror, or refrigerator door so you'll see it, read it, and know it.

The Author

Whatever you can do with horses, Don Blazer has probably done. He isn't one to sit on fences just talking. He always chooses to be part of the action.

He's trained and ridden everything from mustangs to Thoroughbreds, including western and English pleasure horses, reining horses, endurance racers and 300-yard sprinters. He's jumped horses, cut cattle, been over obstacles and around barrels.

He's taught for five colleges and he's traveled from Alaska to Australia demonstrating training techniques at seminars and workshops.

Don is the author of the syndicated column, A Horse, Of Course which is must reading for thousands of fans. He has contributed "how-to" articles to most of the major equine publications and he is a frequent guest on radio talk shows.

Horses he has trained have been to the Quarter Horse World Championships, have won at jumping, dressage and reining, as well as winning Quarter Horse and Thoroughbred stakes races.

Today he keeps busy writing, training and teaching. He lives in Scottsdale, Arizona.

You can do it!

Make Money With Horses

Choose the breed you love, choose doing what you love, then learn to turn protential into profits with weanlings, yearlings, broodmares or stallions. Are you a trainer? Learn how to increase your profit margins and make clients happier. See how fast you can earn by claiming race horses. Know your tax advantages. It's all in **MAKE MONEY WITH HORSES** by Don Blazer.

START SMALL AND GROW AS YOUR EARNINGS INCREASE

The horse industry is a perfect place to create a business on a parttime basis. If you love horses and want them to produce a high standard of living and a quality lifestyle for you, then **TAKE ACTION!**

$19.95 plus $2.50 for shipping

CALL TOLL FREE: **1-888-277-7649** for credit card sales
SEND CHECKS TO: **Success Is Easy**
13610 N. Scottsdale Rd.
Suite 10-406
Scottsdale, AZ 85254
www.donblazer.com

MAKE MONEY WITH HORSES is a practical workbook which tells in simple terms exactly what it takes to enjoy big returns on investment and it gives you absolute rules to follow to be successful.

ALSO AVAILABLE AS AN AUDIO BOOK